Conrad Molden: Collected Essays

War & Peace, Contemporary Politics, Fragile States & Human Security

Contents

What is the *Shadow Economy* of the War in Afghanistan?

"Somehow, in front of our eyes, undeclared wars have been launched in countries across the globe. Foreigners and citizens alike assassinated by presidential decree. The War on Terror transformed into a self fulfilling prophecy. How does a war like this ever end? And what happens to us when we finally see what is hidden in plain sight?" – Jeremy Scahill[1]

'Bin Laden Determined to Strike in the U.S.'
– Title of a memo from the CIA to President Bush, August 6th 2001[2]

i. Introduction

On October 7th 2001, in a televised speech broadcast around the world, President George Bush launched Operation Enduring Freedom. He announced that strategic targets across Afghanistan were to be struck in an effort to disrupt the use of the nation as a terrorist operating base and destabilise the Taliban regime. He ended by noting: "We will not waver; we will not tire; we will not falter; and we will not fail. Peace and freedom will prevail (Bush 2001)." In the twelve years and three months since, the situation has steadily deteriorated. An estimated 21,000 civilians have been killed in the conflict (The Costs of War Project 2013), the UN Office of Drugs and Crime has reported a record high in the cultivation of opium poppies for the production of heroin (BBC News 2013a) and the Taliban still hold incredible power in the region (Sarwary 2012). On May 1st 2012 President Barack Obama signed an agreement to steadily decrease US troop numbers in the region, he stated, "by the end of 2014 the Afghans will be fully responsible for the security of their country (Compton 2012)." Obama claimed: the United States has 'devastated' al Qaeda and prevented them from using Afghanistan to launch attacks against the United States, that the momentum of the Taliban has been broken, and that strong Afghan security forces have been built (Compton: 2012). Ben Anderson argues that, "all it is now is about now is getting out and saving face. We're not leaving because we've achieved our goals, we're leaving because we've given up on achieving those goals... It could even be worse than that because all the fighting has been to introduce a corrupt, hated and feared government who in some areas make the Taliban look like the good guys (Anderson: 2013)." In June 2013 the United States announced its ambition to hold direct talks with the Taliban regime (Roberts 2013). From the initial central objective of destroying the supposedly intolerable Taliban movement,

---

[1] Rowley, R. *Dirty Wars*. 2013. [Film] Big Noise Films.
[2] Suskind, R (2007). *The One Percent Doctrine*. 2nd ed. London: Pocket Books. Pg. 1

the situation twelve years later is a power-sharing agreement, and negotiations, with that very same group.

The Obama administration is facing the harsh reality that stability has not been brought to the region and much like post-2011 Iraq (Otten: 2013), the country may descend into chaos once the troops leave. But has the intervention in Afghanistan been a total loss for every party involved? The Center for International and Strategic Studies estimated in 2014 that the conflict had cost the United States an incredible US$723.9 billion (NPP, 2014). That money has gone into every facet of the war that one would expect: from the armaments and weapons technology, reconstruction projects and building infrastructure, to funding the formation of a state government and paying salaries. It has made a few key institutions in the conflict very wealthy. At the same time, a sinister truth is that foreign assistance could be playing a large role in the funding of the insurgency. The country continues to remain one of the poorest in the world (UNDP 2013), leading to a diversion from failing legal markets to drug cultivation, extortion and illicit tax collection (Nichols 2012). This essay sets to examine precisely what Carolyn Nordstrom describes as a 'shadow economy' and what form it has taken in Afghanistan.

1. Background to Afghanistan

Uzbek, Tajik, Turkmen and Pashtun factions initially occupied the area of South Asia now known as Afghanistan for decades, until state formation formally took place in 1747 (Misdaq: 2006). Of key strategic importance, and with abundance of as-yet unexploited mineral resources, the country has earned a reputation as 'the graveyard of empires' due to a succession of unsuccessful violent occupation attempts. The reasons for intervention in the region have varied; from the conquest of empire by Macedon King Alexander the Great, to a British attempt to influence the region against Russia during the Anglo-Afghan Wars. For the second half of the 20th Century great influence was exerted in the region by both the Soviet Union and the United States. Although the motivations for a US-led intervention in the region are complex and varied, it is worth noting that in January 1998, after negotiations between the then-governing Taliban and American petroleum explorer Unocal Corporation, the construction of a 1700km pipeline began from the Caspian Sea in Turkmenistan to India through Afghanistan and Pakistan (BBC News: 2002). Seven months later Taliban-linked Saudi Osama bin Laden was accused of orchestrating a series of bombings at US embassies in East

Africa, after which pipeline construction was frozen. The failure of the US to bring stability to the region means it is as difficult as ever to build through areas of Afghanistan and Pakistan that are not controlled by their state governments, and as such the pipeline is still incomplete. Pilger argues that lobbying from enormous oil corporations who have investments in the project, such as British Petroleum, ExxonMobil[3] and Chevron, could have played a large role in the decision to go to war (2002). Møller argues, "[States have] frequently gone to war to enrich themselves… or in order to enforce favourable conditions for their economic ventures (2002)." It is very difficult to point to any particular potential motivation for the War in Afghanistan, such as the Trans-Afghanistan Pipeline, and say with any precision how influential it has been. As Klein argues, "the people involved are notorious for conflating corporate interests with national interest, to the extent that they themselves are seemingly incapable of drawing distinctions (Klein 2008: 309)." What is recognisable in Afghanistan is that a complex network of actors are attempting to influence political decisions when outcomes could be highly beneficial. The collapse of law and order, compounded by relentless fighting, has created an 'artificial' economy heavily dependent on foreign aid (Mallet 2013) which has allowed lucrative and controversial markets to flourish.

2. The Shadow Economy

Nordstrom refers to a 'shadow economy' as "the complex set of cross-state economic and political linkages that move outside formally recognised state-based channels… the transactions defining these networks aren't confined solely to criminal, illicit, or illegal activities, but cross various divides between legal, quasi-legal, and downright illegal activities (Nordstrom 2004: 106)." The recognition that warfare especially produces a space in which the legality of transactions are difficult to define is an important one. Profiteering from warfare is certainly nothing new to the 21st Century. Where groups have existed wishing to wage war there have been suppliers to meet demand. What is significant about Afghanistan is its evolved nature into what Kaldor describes as a 'New War'. She writes, "[new wars] occur in the context of the erosion of the monopoly of legitimate organized violence (1998: 5)." Operation Enduring Freedom does not fit into the archetypal understandings of nation-state based conflict, but rather an intervention in a fragmented society to alter a wide variety of structures. Kaldor argues that political legitimacy disappears when violence is privatised by the growth of

---

[3] The third largest company in the world by revenue.

organised crime and paramilitary groups (1998). In Afghanistan this has taken the form of two distinct actions by coalition forces, both invested with vast amounts of financial support, and both major components of the conflict: contraction of services to private military companies and the funding of warlords.

2.1 Private Military Companies

The arms industry has a global estimated annual worth of between 350 and US$500 billion[4] (Smith 2013), in 2012 it represented nearly 4.5% of the USA's GDP (World Bank 2013). A report by the Congressional Research Service found that as of March 2011 there were "more contractor personnel in Afghanistan and Iraq (155,000) than uniformed personnel (145,000) (Congressional Research Service 2011)". The US Department of Defense stated in November 2012 that in the last quarter of the year there were over 109,000 contractors in Afghanistan, nearly double the number of US troops (Loewenstein 2013: 138). This figure does not include the contractors operating on agreements with other agencies (Dickinson 2011: 189). A third of all these contracts, supplied by the United States Department of Defense, have gone to just five major companies, the five largest defence contractors in the United States (Eloise 2012): Lockheed Martin, Boeing Company, Northrop Grumman Corporation, Raytheon and General Dynamics (The Costs of War Project 2013). Together they have made vast sums of money from the US' decision to invade and occupy Afghanistan. Nordstrom asks, "why can one see the same international cast of business people, profiteers and black-marketeers transporting these war-related supplies across the war zones of the world? (Nordstrom 2004: 93)." These companies aren't only operating in this conflict, but around the world, coming to the rescue of governments and military groups desperate for weapons, training and logistics. Melman describes a war economy as "one in which military spending is a continuing, significant and legitimate end-purpose of economic activity (1985: 260)." The businesses operating in Afghanistan are motivated by profit, and as long as the conflict continues they earn from the government's dependence on them. These companies too, support in direct combat and advise military strategy (Isenberg 2010). For example, in Autumn 2008 the US State Department tasked DynCorp International with a US$317.4 million order requesting 'police advisors' to assist in training sessions in Afghanistan for a period of eighteen months (Dickinson 2011: 138). Møller argues that the distinction between mercenaries from private military

---

[4] Roughly 2.7 trillion Danish krone.

companies is not only their corporate nature, but also the diversification of their activities. PMCs do "not merely engage in combat, but also in a wide range of other military activities such as training and logistics (Møller 2005: 15)" and form parts of companies who have subsidiaries involved in non-military sectors. These companies are huge complex constructions with investments in many aspects of the conflict, and the desire to have their services preserved. Loewenstein argues, "Afghanistan was a veritable blank slate on which a new society could be drawn purely to benefit the bottom lines of corporations that sell themselves as essential to the war effort… It is this environment, combined with minimal media scrutiny and limited public knowledge of PMCs, which has allowed this aspect of *vulture capitalism* to flourish in US war zones over the past twelve years (Loewenstein 2013: 141)."

The motivations for the privatisation of the conflict centre around improving efficiency, cutting costs (Loewenstein 2013: 133) and securing the manpower necessary to occupy South Asia; as Stanger argues: "without contractors, we would need a draft to wage these two wars (2011)." Either set out with positive intentions, or ready to exploit an opportunity, both the bestowing and completing of contracts has not only created an arena for profit in an otherwise disastrous situation, but has too made its perpetuation all the more comfortable for a government in need of aid from multinational corporations. Klein asserts, "the Bush administration immediately seized upon the fear generated by the [September 11th] attacks not only to launch the 'War on Terror' but to ensure that it is an almost completely for-profit venture, a booming new industry that has breathed new life into the faltering U.S. economy… The ultimate goal for the corporations at the center of the complex is to bring the model of for-profit government, which advances so rapidly in extraordinary circumstances, into the ordinary and day-to-day functioning of the state – in effect, to privatize the government (Klein 2008: 12)."

2.2 Funding Warlords

The Taliban originated in 1991, grown from the need to begin enforcing law and order in a region of Afghanistan decimated by the Soviet invasion. Nordstrom argues, "the more formal nature of state-based systems is vulnerable to bureaucratic gridlock, while non-formal systems can more easily and flexibly meet demands (2004: 103)."

By contributing much needed services and building a political community the Taliban provided a practical alternative during the ensuing Afghan Civil War. The same situation of informal non-state paramilitaries gaining power from desperate communities has occurred since 2001: "Despite all the loud promises of aid and assistance being made internationally, the Afghan people see little evidence of it on the ground. Partially as a result of this, the warlords are regaining their hold over the country because they appear to some people to offer the best options for employment, and individual advancement (Bell; Langlands 2004)." Nordstrom asserts, "guerrilla warfare uses political control of the population... By capturing hearts and minds the strategic goal... is to mobilise extremist politics based on fear and hatred (2004: 8 - 9)." In a failed state it is not enough to simply replace the already illegitimately perceived government. Those who win favour are the ones meeting the needs of the population and filling a power vacuum, even if the average citizen disagrees with them ideologically. The notion that in 2001 thirty million people could be willed to simply oppose a long-established previously-supported regime without a viable alternative was a fiction.

Since control was taken in the 1980s by the US-backed *mujahideen* (Johnson 2004: 90) opium cultivation for heroin production has proven to be a lucrative cash crop in Afghanistan. It is now the nation's leading economic activity, in some instances yielding five times the market wage rate for the same level of unskilled labour (World Bank 2005: 113). Failure to bring stability to the region has meant a suffering economy that not only allows for the drug trade to flourish as a fruitful substitute but gives criminals already engaged in the practice further financing.

The United States too have been involved in the direct funding of warlords. "[The Bush administration] had for all intents and purposes divided Afghanistan three ways. The north was given to an infamous Uzbek warlord Rashid Dostum; the west to another warlord, Ismail Khan and Kabul to [President Hamid] Karzai (Misdaq 2006: 252)." Despite all the US' claims that an effective government has been installed, the unfortunate situation is that they have, in accordance with their objective to 'strengthen forces hostile to the Taliban regime' (Misdaq 2006: 254), given vast amounts of funding to warlords. The "ISAF [International Security Force for Afghanistan][5] only operates in Kabul. With the exception of Kandahar, where the US battle group hunting the Taliban and al Qaeda remnants is based, the rest of Afghanistan is still controlled entirely by warlords and their local commanders (Bell; Langlands 2004)." To protect supply routes and limit the capacity of the Taliban, it is estimated that the Department

---

[5] The NATO-derived multinational taskforce.

of Defense has paid at least 10% of its logistics contracts, worth hundreds of millions of dollars, to insurgents (Roston 2009).

3. Outcomes

The invasion of Afghanistan came only twenty-six days after the September 11th attacks, at a time when the United States was in mourning and a thorough investigation had yet to commence. "The West needed a narrative to justify war… this was to be a humanitarian war, a war fought only for the best of motives and with the best of intentions. For this it was necessary that the Taliban were portrayed as the personification of evil, and Afghans, particularly women, as their victims… the media coverage created a picture of a regime that was unremittingly brutal and from which its people had to be rescued (Johnson: 2004)." What has materialised in Afghanistan is what Loewenstein refers to as a 'laboratory' for research into privatised military and intelligence (2013: 160). The correct combination of war justifications, military contracts and big business interests has provided the shadows in which a new controversial economy has been built.

Former-CIA agent Bruce Riedel claims, "defeat is what we were staring in the eye two years ago [2006]. Catastrophic defeat in Afghanistan, with the Taliban taking over the southern half of the country and maybe being able to march on Kabul at some point (Blair: 2011)." As a foreboding this is almost precisely the situation Afghanistan finds itself in today, without a coherent central government and anticipating the looming US withdrawal. Anderson argues, "after all this money and effort and bloodshed, all we're saying to villagers... is, we'll give you a weapon and you can defend yourself. So we're asking Afghans to pick sides on the side of the Afghan government right as we're leaving and right as the Taliban are as strong as ever. And if I was an Afghan living in Helmand province I wouldn't pick any side, I'd be nice to whichever strongman was in my garden at that point (Anderson 2013)." It isn't just a lack of faith in the government that is troubling, but overwhelming reports of the Afghan National Security Forces (ANSF) engaging in corruption, kidnapping, drug use, murder and child abuse (BBC 2013b). Organisations funded, trained and endorsed by Western nations are acting as immorally as many of the other competing factions in a lawless land. Riedel claims that at the start of the invasion, "[the United States government] sent in twenty or thirty CIA officers with several million dollars in 'walking around' money and bought the Northern Alliance (Blair 2004)." What followed is the Northern Alliance, a military front formed in 1996 with a strong alliance to the United States, has now effectively been legitimised as the national afghan security with responsibility for the army and police. The ANSF are comprised predominantly of ethnic groups from the northern regions of Afghanistan, where the United States has been most successful at gaining control; while the Pashtun ethnic group, which comprise 42% of the total population (CIA 2013) and is based mainly in the south where the Taliban originated and is strongest, are almost entirely excluded from proceedings (Anderson 2013). At a House Armed Services Committee Vanda Brown testified that in Afghanistan, "murder, extortion, and land theft have gone unpunished, often perpetrated by those in the government. At the same time, access to jobs, promotions, and economic rents has depended on being on good terms with the local strongman, instead of merit and hard work (2012)." Major Bill Steuber, part of an advisory team training the Afghan National Police, argues that the US forces have to be much more lenient with the Afghani forces than they would with their own soldiers: "In order to get the mission accomplished, in order for them to actually go out and still hold security, still hold PBs [Patrol Bases], you've got to let it go. If we were to go in and shut down all of their schemes, all of their corruption schemes, you would render them completely ineffective (Anderson 2013)."

Where the United States has failed to instigate law and order desperate people have had their needs compounded by relentless violence and the blatant empowering of vicious groups by occupying forces. Former US Ambassador to Afghanistan Karl Eikenberry claims: "we aligned ourselves with warlords, and our objective was to destroy al Qaeda, and we then very-much created and empowered a group of political actors [who are] not accountable… as they grew in power [they] actually created more instability (Blair: 2011)."

4. Conclusion

Afghanistan "has a reputation as being the last nail in the coffin of empires that have overstretched themselves (Misdaq 2006: 267)." For the United States the cost has not only been paid by average American citizens through their taxes and adoption of US government debt, but in the lives of the 2300 men and women who have been killed in combat (iCasualties 2014). The UN estimates that over 3250 foreign soldiers have also perished, along with thousands of contractors, many of who go unreported (Loewenstein 2013: 140).

Ultimately it is the deaths of 21000 Afghan civilians (The Costs of War Project 2013), which summarise what the war has accomplished. Not only through aerial strikes, collateral damage and incorrect identifications, but too by killing those who defended against their occupation. Chief of the General Staff Richard Dannatt claims, "a lot of the people we were killing were effectively the farmers who had AK47s put in their hands by the Taliban leadership. 'Part-time Talibs', and not very well trained ones, and we killed huge numbers of them (Blair: 2011)." The murdering of a family member not only does immeasurable damage to a community, but it solidly undermines the intentions of the invading force; resistance in Afghanistan has been fierce not least because of the high civilian casualty rate.

Where the shadow economy has stepped in enormous profits have been extracted from an otherwise devastating time in one of the poorest countries in the world. Collier argues, "if economic agendas are driving conflict, then it is likely that some groups are benefiting from conflict and that these groups therefore have some interest in initiating and sustaining it (2000: 91)." The companies, warlords and drug traders set to gain from the conflict have welcomed its conservation. This has begun the process of merging profit-incentives with the stated objectives of, amongst other things, destroying al Qaeda's infrastructure and establish a US-friendly government (Misdaq 2006: 254). Prado argues that the conflict has allowed for the collusion of international security companies in government corruption and illegal businesses, "included creating insecurity with the objective of securing their business and expanding contracts by providing anti-government groups with bribes… providing havens for suspects or alleged perpetrators of human rights violations and crimes against humanity (Prado: 2013)."

In 2012 the US Geological Society confirmed that Afghanistan has vast amounts of mineral resources, huge untapped reserves of everything from precious metals to fossil fuels, with an estimated value that runs into the trillions (Loewenstein 2013: 154). As the overt US presence prepares to wind down by 2014 the fear is that Afghanistan will be shaped, like many battlegrounds of the War on Terror, by the victors of the ensuing power vacuum. The possibility of further collapse into civil war is palpable, one that may be horribly moulded by a scramble to find profit in the debris.

The objectives of the United States have not been met and the region has potentially been made more volatile. The shadow economy of the conflict in Afghanistan has been far reaching, giving traction to industries built on the permanence of war and aiding those who battle with the United States. Reflecting on the evolution of post-September 11 conflicts Klein writes, "the primary economic role of wars, however, was as a means to open new markets that had been sealed off and to generate postwar peacetime booms. Now wars and disaster responses are so fully privatized that they are themselves the new market; there is no need to wait until after the war for the boom – the medium is the message (Klein 2008: 13)."

Appendix A.

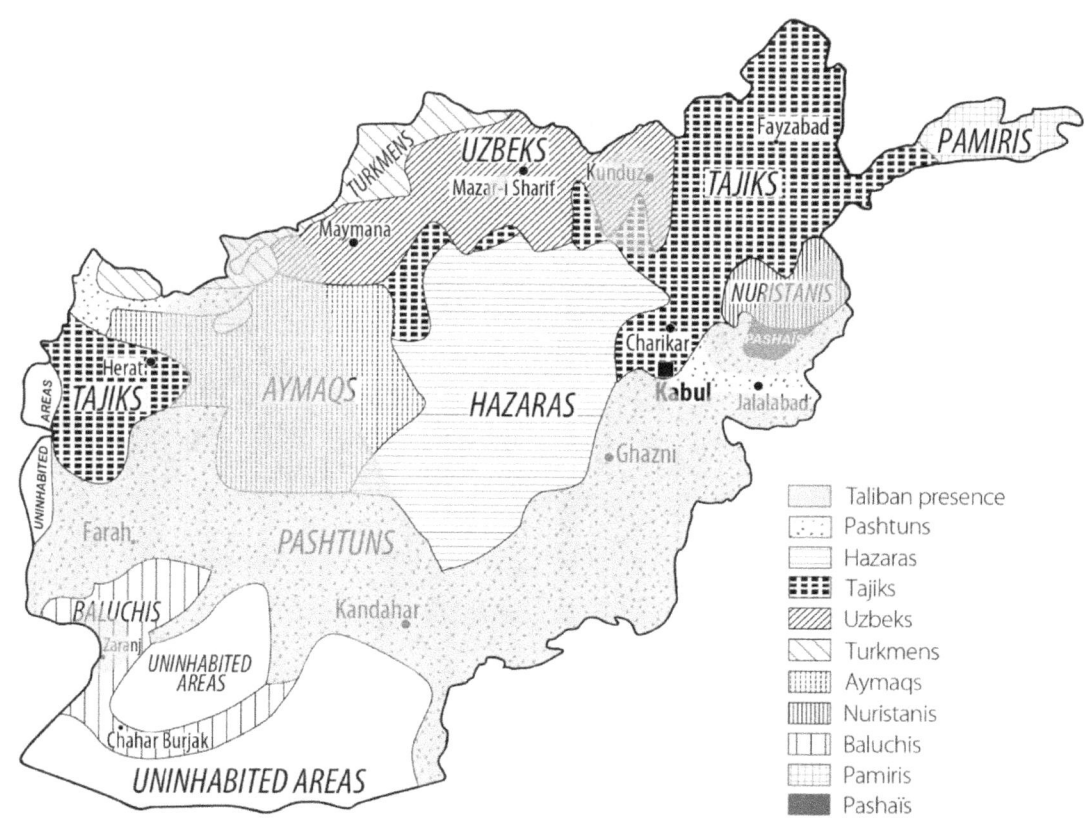

Ethnicities and Taliban presence in Afghanistan, 2009.

Appendix B.

Taliban forces gathered in Pakistan, 2004.
Still from Blair's documentary *Afghanistan: War Without End* (2004).

Coalition military casualties in Afghanistan by month

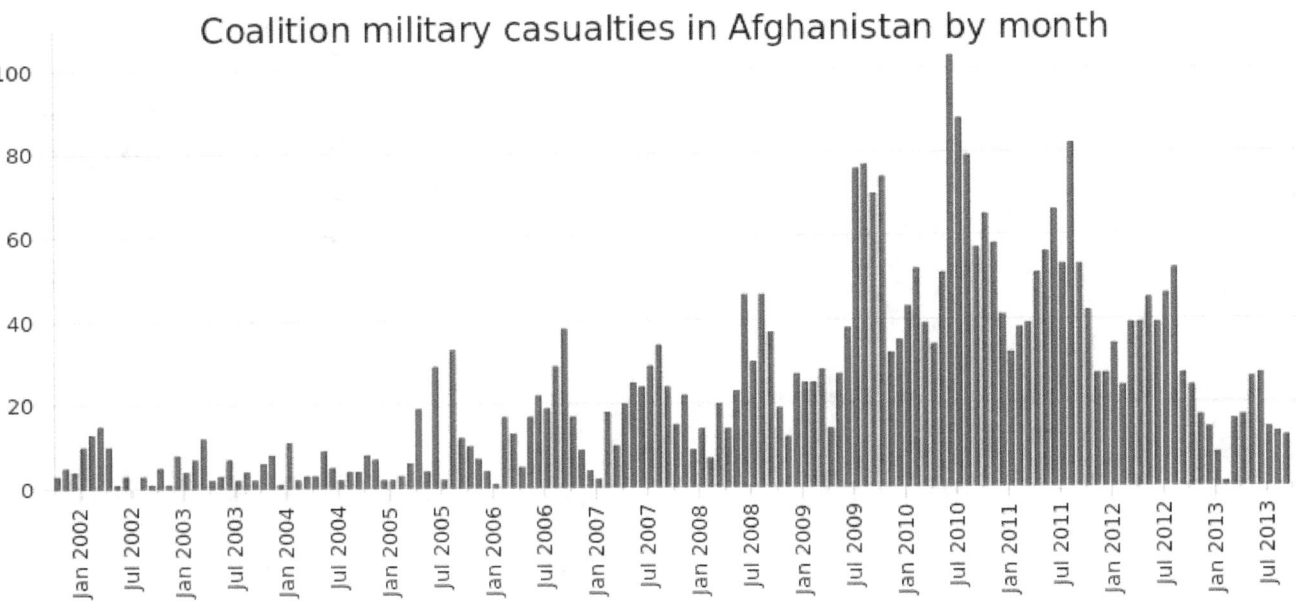

Appendix D.

![Still from documentary showing British forces in Helmand Province]

"He was so stoned that he went outside, stood up in full view of the Taliban, aimed into the sky. A bullet fired the magazine off of his gun and he just picked it up off the ground, laughed and walked back inside."

British forces fighting alongside the Afghan National Army in Helmand Province.
Still from Anderson's documentary *Inside Afghanistan* (2008).

Appendix E.

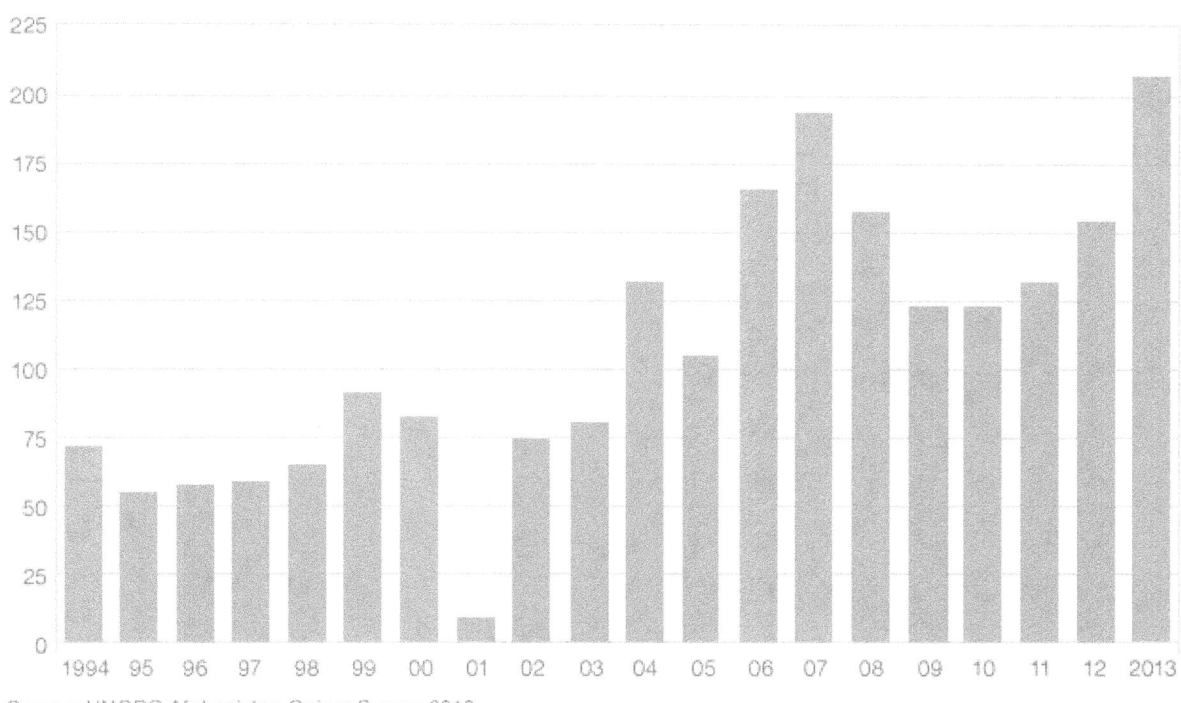

Opium cultivation in Afghanistan, 1994-2013

Hectares (thousands)

Source: UNODC Afghanistan Opium Survey 2013

Appendix F. Courtesy of *BBC News / Reuters*

June 6th 2014. The front-runner in Afghan's presidential election, Abdullah Abdullah survives a suspected Taliban-alliance suicide bomb attack targeted at his convoy in Kabul.

"Many observers now believe that future peace in Afghanistan can only come if the government in Kabul negotiates with the Taliban."

What is the relationship between poverty, warfare and the International Monetary Fund?

"If we really want to get to the root cause of poverty – not just its surface manifestations – we must commit ourselves to a larger and more long-term struggle than simply handing out relief supplies. You can rescue every drowning child out of the river, but if you don't go upstream to stop the guy who's throwing the kids in the water in the first place, you'll never get a real solution."[6] - Activist Kevin Danaher

"It is no coincidence that the century of total war coincided with the century of central banking."[7]

- United States Congressman Ron Paul

On the northern coast of Jamaica, just outside of the second-largest city of the island nation is the sprawling site of Montego Bay Free Zone. The complex covers 380,000 square meters, with over 45,000 of them dedicated to factory space alone.[8] Within its walls are thousands of Jamaican nationals and foreign workers completing tasks such as operating sewing machines, driving forklift trucks or standing at conveyor belts packing boxes, in a vast network that is involved in every kind of field from manufacturing and processing to refining and packaging. Companies like Tommy Hilfiger Corporation, Brooks Brothers and HanesBrands Inc. employ thousands of people for as little as US$30 for five days of work,[9] to get their products onto market. The Montego Bay Free Zone, along with five others like it in Jamaica, operates as though the goods they process never entered the country. Ships carrying containers make the deliveries; the goods are then passed through guarded gates into the factories, processed, and placed back onto the ships to continue their journey without interference from customs authorities. This protocol means that companies are not liable to local controls such as income tax, excise or importing licenses. The zones are specifically designed to entice foreign investment and international trade, but 85% of all goods leaving them must go to nations outside those fifteen that make up the Caribbean Community (CARICOM). All these are measures imposed by the International Monetary Fund (IMF) and the World Bank in loan agreements the country took out over a series of years to a total of US$4.5 billion.[10] The story of Jamaica is one of a nation that found itself in economic difficulties following its

---

[6] Danaher, K (2001). *10 Reasons to Abolish the IMF and World Bank*. Washington D.C.: Seven Stories Press. Pg. 18
[7] Paul, R (2010). *End The Fed*. Hachette Book Group: Grand Central Publishing. Pg. 63
[8] American University Washington D.C.. (2012). *Jamaica: IT Geographics*. Available: http://www1.american.edu/initeb/js1513a/geo.htm. Last accessed 28th Jan 2012.
[9] US$30 before tax.
[10] Stephanie Black. (2002). *About Life and Debt*. Available: http://www.lifeanddebt.org/about.html. Last accessed 1st Feb 2012.

independence from British rule in 1962, and due to its instability was unable to receive a loan from a private bank and could only appeal to the IMF. The loans were given under the condition that the country would radically alter its fiscal and monetary systems; former-Chief Economist of the World Bank and current Governor of the Bank of Israel, Stanley Fischer justified this in 1991: "Jamaica is a very small country, it's not a country which could thrive by producing only for itself. We [the IMF] believe very firmly that countries are going to grow better if they're integrated into the world economy and that means reducing tariffs. And it needed to allow its importers, it's people, access to goods from the rest of the world rather than having to rely on this little economy."[11] In an attempt to encourage growth in the Jamaican economy the IMF policies proved to do the reverse, flooding the market with imported goods, leaving fertile land abandoned, sending prices soaring and killing local business. By the end of the agreed loan period 63% of all the IMF's proposed conditions had been implemented upon Jamaica,[12] and following calls for an investigation into sixteen years of the IMF policies' effects, a report from the Office of the Director-General of the World Bank reported that "in the end, the [Jamaican] economy achieved neither growth nor poverty reduction."[13]

This essay is not a critique of laissez-faire capitalism, or of Libertarianism and free markets. Rather it is a critical analysis of the International Monetary Fund, an organisation that directly affects the economies of over 184 countries worldwide and is basically "the single most powerful non-state (governance) institution in the world."[14] It is an organisation that influences the lives of billions of people through funds it seizes from taxpayers of member nations, investments made without democratic process and by commanding the returns to private investors. This essay will examine the intentions of the IMF, the effects of its policies upon the nations it loans to and will understand its policies as a new kind of economic warfare, one that has the symptoms of conventional violent conflict but with subtle process.

---

[11] *Life and Debt*, 2001. [DVD] Stephanie Black, USA: Tuff Gong Pictures.
[12] Mosley, P (1995). *Aid and Power*. London: Routledge. Pg. 142
[13] The World Bank. (1998). *Jamaica: Country Assistance Note*. Available: www-wds.worldbank.org/external/default/WDSContentServer/WDSP/IB/1999/07/22/000094946_99062505423382/Rendered/PDF/multi_page.pdf. Last accessed 29th Jan 2012. Pg. 1
[14] Peet, R (2005). *Unholy Trinity*. 3rd ed. New York: Zed Books Ltd. Pg. 56

The Birth of the International Monetary Fund and its Intentions

The United Nations Monetary and Financial Conference[15] was held at the beginning of July 1944 by representatives from forty-four countries, and spearheaded by the interests on the United States and the United Kingdom.[16] One of the major goals of the gathering was the formation of organisations that would aid post-Second World War reconstruction as an Allied victory was becoming clear. Former Prime Minister of Jamaica, Michael Manley, argues that 'the third world' was not represented at the conference, the decisions made were made by an elite who commanded global empires, and those interests were the ones being served by the decisions made.[17] Author Naomi Klein describes the institutions formed under the Bretton Woods system, and their successor, the World Trade Organization, as international institutions with an ideology conceived by 'corporate interests' and enforced by 'national politicians'.[18] The World Bank[19] was initially envisaged as a long-term investment bank, with the IMF formed as a "permanent institution to promote international monetary cooperation and provide the machinery through which countries could consult and collaborate,"[20] essentially aiding temporary relief to nations in need of liquidity. During its first thirty years the IMF succeeded in providing short-term loans to 'developed' nations on an 'as needed' basis, stabilising temporary financial hardship.[21] Following the 1973 Oil Crisis, under Richard Nixon the United States took itself out from the Bretton Woods Accord and the IMF turned its attention towards loaning to heavily indebted nations.[22] Following its collapse, "the Bretton Woods system was replaced by a much looser set of international monetary arrangements. There was very little 'system' left, and, in effect, the international monetary system was privatized, with the result that there was no clear-cut role for a quasi-government institution such as the Fund."[23] This left the relationship between the IMF and the United Nations significantly altered. According to Articles 63 of the UN Charter, the United Nations Economic and Social Council (ECOSOC), accountable to the UN General Assembly, should be in control of both the World Bank and International

---

[15] Better known as the Bretton Woods Conference.

[16] Peet, R (2005). *Unholy Trinity*. 3rd ed. New York: Zed Books Ltd. Pg. 27

[17] *Life and Debt*, 2001. [DVD] Stephanie Black, USA: Tuff Gong Pictures.

[18] Klein, N (2002). *Fences and Windows*. London: HarperCollins Publishers Inc. Pg. xv

[19] Initially conceived of as the International Bank of Reconstruction and Development (IBRD).

[20] Peet, R (2005). *Unholy Trinity*. 3rd ed. New York: Zed Books Ltd. Pg. 49

[21] Browne, R (1994). *Beyond Bretton Woods*. London: Pluto Press. Pg. 57

[22] *Ibid*. Pg. 60

[23] Bird, G (1995). *IMF Lending to Developing Countries*. London: Routledge. Pg. 3

Monetary Fund, as they "co-ordinate the activities of the specialized agencies through consultation with and recommendations to such agencies."[24] Although this is originally how the hierarchy was set out, following the changes of the 1970s, neither of these institutions continued to operate under United Nations control, and as such are only accountable to first-world banking interests who operate them, especially with regard to the free-market ideologies they espouse.[25]

Policy and Conclusion

The IMF provides liquidity to nations in crisis and facing exogenous shocks, but it does so through a very particular criteria embodied in its Structural Adjustment Programmes (SAPs), advising its borrowers, not only in order that they repay, but to "reform the deep microstructure of their economies."[26] Attached to their loan agreements both the IMF and the World Bank have a set of stipulations. These include, but are not limited to: the 'liberalisation' of trade including the removal of restrictions on foreign investment, and allowing repatriation of profits; radical reduction on public spending including health, welfare and education; privatisation and deregulation of state-controlled enterprises; reduction in wages and elimination or weakening of labour protections; and the devaluation of the nation's currency.[27]

The devaluing of the nations currency comes in the form of inflation, or "an increase in the amount of money in circulation not backed by the monetary commodity,"[28][29] a tactic believed by the IMF to stimulate imports and diminish exports. In the case of Jamaica, beginning with the IMF involvement in 1977, the devaluing of the currency very quickly caused prices to rise.[30] This was an inevitable consequence of the intentional inflationary measures, the upward pressure applied to prices comes, because "more money is chasing an unchanged supply of goods, buyers are able and willing to pay more for them, giving sellers in turn the ability to charge more."[31] The dilution of the value of each monetary unit in circulation, following inflationary measures, takes time and is unequal. Those who benefit most are those who receive the

---

[24] United Nations. (2012). *Charter of the United Nations: Chapter 10.* Available: http://www.un.org/en/documents/charter/chapter10.shtml. Last accessed 1st Feb 2012.
[25] Fulcher, J (2004). *Capitalism.* New York: Oxford University Press. Pg. 100
[26] Tandon, Y (2008). *Ending Aid Dependence.* Oxford: Fahamu Books. Pg. 62
[27] Tandon, Y (2008). *Ending Aid Dependence.* Oxford: Fahamu Books. Pg. 45
[28] Woods, T (2009). *Meltdown.* Washington D.C.: Regnery Publishing Inc. Pg. 121
[29] An increase in paper note claims to gold that are not backed by increases in gold itself.
[30] *Life and Debt,* 2001. [DVD] Stephanie Black, USA: Tuff Gong Pictures.
[31] Woods, T (2009). *Meltdown.* Washington D.C.: Regnery Publishing Inc. Pg. 122

money first, such as the large conglomerates who received funds straight from the government and descended upon the small Caribbean island. They benefitted at the loss of those who received the newly created paper money last, those on fixed incomes like teachers, landowners with long-term leases and pensioners.[32] The measures taken to encourage the import of goods did work, but not with the results stated by the IMF loan agreement. When Jamaica was opened up to the global market, imports of cheaper produce did flood the island as intended. This meant that although produce was now substantially cheaper for the average consumer, the agricultural industry was all but eradicated overnight. Although the IMF enforces a ban upon subsidisation of industry, many other nations including the United States do not commit to the same ideal, and certain companies were very easily able to undercut the local Jamaican produce. Unable to compete, local farms closed or went bankrupt altogether and unemployment rose.[33] This policy was of great detriment to the people of Jamaica, and was only compounded by the IMF's other austerity policy, to "reduce wasteful government spending."[34] The welfare that would have been in place to insure that those people in financial difficulties would be saved from poverty had been removed. The breaking point came in April of 1997 when the price of petroleum increased 30% and riots broke out across the country, resulting in the destruction of property, attacks on civilians and the killing of 149 people by armed police.[35] Where the IMF has claimed it will administer policy to the poorest and most desperate nations to build economies which create prosperity and lift nations out of poverty, "these projects have been a boon to multinational mining, textile, and agribusiness companies around the world, but in many countries they have also led to environmental devastation, mass migration to urban centres, currency crashes and dead-end sweatshop jobs."[36]

In the 1990s the IMF placed the government of Thailand under pressure to 'liberalise' capital flows in and out of the country. The collateral used by many private businesses to obtain loans had largely been based on property that had an inflated value, due to speculation and malinvestment caused by the central bank. When this Asian property bubble burst in August 1997 banks recalled their loans and the private sector defaulted.

---

[32] Rothbard, M (2011). *What Has Government Done to Our Money?*. New York: Terra Libertas Limited. Pg. 53

[33] *Life and Debt*, 2001. [DVD] Stephanie Black, USA: Tuff Gong Pictures.

[34] Fulcher, J (2004). *Capitalism*. New York: Oxford University Press. Pg. 101

[35] Amnesty International. (2001). *Jamaica: Killings and Violence by Police*. Available: http://www.amnesty-caribbean.org/Jamaica/AMR3800101/bericht.htm. Last accessed 1st Feb 2012.

[36] Klein, N (2002). *Fences and Windows*. London: HarperCollins Publishers Inc. Pg. 9

As the Bank of Thailand desperately tried to sell resources to maintain the currency's value, it led to the liquidation of many banks and ultimately the bailing out of those banks by the Thai taxpayer, meaning, "private debts were transformed into public debts."[37] What became known as the '1997 Asian Financial Crisis' spread from Thailand to South Korea, the Philippines, Malaysia and devastated Indonesia.

In January 1998 President Suharto of Indonesia signed an IMF agreement, receiving a massive loan to stabilise the collapsing economy. Briefly the situation settled, before suddenly the economy crashed disastrously as the currency rapidly devalued by 80%.[38] As prices soared so did unemployment, people were unable to seek welfare because that had been removed from the budget and rioting ensued. Critics of the IMF and United States Secretary of the Treasury Robert Rubin, began arguing that the billions of dollars paid into the Asian banks had been used to pay the debt owed to Western investors who had suffered from the depression. The funds had been given to benefit those invested corporations, which had caused the temporary settlement, but once that had occurred the economy had crashed.[39] It became clear that the intention of the IMF had not been to aid the indebted citizens of Thailand but "to bail out hard-pressed American financial and banking interests, and to create conditions for further control by American (and allies') capital over the national economies of the developing countries in distress."[40] Without constraint the IMF was able to invest funds that saved private interests from insolvency, leaving the people of an entire nation with the debt burden. This process has left the organisation working against the people it had been established to protect, benefiting 'Wall Street insiders' instead of citizens of developing nations.[41] Anti-globalisation activist Kevin Danaher argues that the global economic policy instigated by the IMF "is made through an institutional web of collaborators by élites, dominated by the lenders of the major industrial countries."[42] This 'revolving door' between administering policy and financially benefitting from those decisions outside of office comes in the form of many individuals. Amongst them James Baker, former Secretary of the Treasury, who administered policy for the

---

[37] Tandon, Y (2008). *Ending Aid Dependence*. Oxford: Fahamu Books. Pg. 59

[38] *All Watched Over by Machines of Loving Grace, Episode 1: Love and Power*, 2011. [DVD] Adam Curtis, United Kingdom: BBC Productions.

[39] *Ibid.*

[40] Tandon, Y (2008). *Ending Aid Dependence*. Oxford: Fahamu Books. Pg. 62

[41] Fulcher, J (2004). *Capitalism: A Very Short Introduction*. New York: Oxford University Press. Pg. 101

[42] Danaher, K (2001). *10 Reasons to Abolish the IMF and World Bank*. Washington D.C.: Seven Stories Press. Pg. 9

IMF and went on to become a senior counsellor at the Carlyle Group, an asset management firm who benefit from those same funds.[43] William Simon, former Secretary of the Treasury, sat on the Board of Governors at both the IMF and the World Bank, and would receive profits from investments made possible by those organisations when later working for the investment-banking firm Salomon Brothers.[44] Many others, including Secretaries of Commerce and members of the IMF have gone on to profit personally from their ability to invest in companies that benefit from those policy decisions.

Professor Hedley Bull describes warfare as "organised violence carried on by political units against each other."[45] As has been demonstrated, the IMF can restrict the sovereignty of a state to dictate its own financial affairs and prevent it developing as it deems fit. It produces the effects of warfare, in Thailand it "destroyed wealth on a massive scale and sent absolute poverty shooting up… Corporate loans equivalent to around half of one year's GDP went bad – a destruction of savings on a scale more usually associated with a full scale war."[46] Investigative journalist John Pilger describes the work of the IMF as 'war by other means'.[47] He spoke about his visit to the World Bank and International Monetary Fund Conference in Bangkok, Thailand in 1991: "The aim of the conference is, and I quote 'to find ways of eradicating poverty all over the world'. Alas, there are contradictions… most of the delegates are bankers, now this is not to suggest that bankers don't care about poor people, it is just that some things are hard to explain. Such as, why officials of the World Bank spend, in pursuit of their solutions for the poor, and estimated $45 million a year flying first class and staying in five-star hotels. And why at this conference are chefs being flown in especially from Paris to a country where children still die from malnutrition."[48]

Self-confessed 'economic hit man' John Perkins is correct to describe the IMF and the World Bank as "a symbiotic relationship developed between governments, corporations, and multilateral organizations."[49] Their policies of 'trade liberalisation' have not reduced poverty by redistributing wealth "but in fact further widening the gap

---

[43] Klein, N (2008). *The Shock Doctrine*. 2nd ed. London: Penguin Group. Pg. 317

[44] Peet, R (2005). *Unholy Trinity*. 3rd ed. New York: Zed Books Ltd. Pg. 207-208

[45] Speller, I (2008). *Understanding Modern Warfare*. Cambridge: Cambridge University Press. Pg. 1

[46] The Economist, 8th February 2003, *The East Asian Crisis*, Pg. 15

[47] *War By Other Means*, 1992. [DVD] David Munro, United Kingdom: Central Independent Television plc.

[48] *Ibid.*

[49] Perkins, J (2005). *Confessions of an Economic Hit Man*. London: Ebury Press. Pg. 19

between the rich and poor in all nations."[50] They have caused the disruption and destruction expected of conventional warfare, through the guise of humanitarian aid, and promises of a better future. "The World Bank and the IMF are the two most powerful enforcers of the growth ideology and a system of measurement that hides the social and environmental costs of market-led growth."[51]

---

[50] Danaher, K (2001). *10 Reasons to Abolish the IMF and World Bank*. Washington D.C.: Seven Stories Press. Pg. 15

[51] Danaher, K (2001). *10 Reasons to Abolish the IMF and World Bank*. Washington D.C.: Seven Stories Press. Pg. 36

What hangs on the question 'is the Holocaust unique?' Is it unique?

"Upon arrival, the deportees are immediately referred to as 'pezzi' (pieces), denying their humanity, whilst the obliteration of identity through the removal of personal names, and their replacement with a tattooed number, indelibly marks them as subhuman masses, like beasts destined for the slaughterhouse."[52]

In September 1939, following the invasion of Poland by Nazi Germany, Rudolf Höss was appointed as first commandant of Auschwitz concentration camp. It is documented that in the camp's infancy he would personally have to drive up to sixty miles to obtain much needed resources for operations that took place there.[53] In the next six years the camp would develop beyond a series of buildings for political prisoners and grow to become part of a network of camps and factories[54], which would be used to murder over 9 million people.[55] Auschwitz Birkenau, the largest concentration camp under Nazi control, has become a symbol of what the Holocaust embodied. The industrial manner by which millions of individuals were systematically murdered by state-sponsored organisations asks questions of how this particular genocide relates to the rest of history, in particular the Holocaust's description as a 'unique' event.

This essay sets to examine what exactly 'the Holocaust' was and how interpretations of the event lead to different understandings of its relation to other genocides. It will examine events within the genocide and relate them to understandings of its 'uniqueness' and ask what conclusions can be drawn from the question 'is the Holocaust unique?'

It is an obvious and self-evident claim that everything is unique, for no two basic units of matter can exist that are entirely identical and as such no compounds of those units can create any two items that are entirely identical. The uniqueness debate does not examine the Holocaust as a truism. The idea that the Holocaust is unique centres on the appropriation that it is incomparable to anything else and as such is outside of categorisation. It is also considered that the Holocaust can not occur again if it is unique, the factors that led to the actions taken can not be replicated. There are two starting points from which to ask if the Holocaust is unique, the first is of empirical fact.

The United Nations defines genocide as "acts committed with intent to destroy, in

---

[52] Benchouiha, L (2006). *Primo Levi: Rewriting the Holocaust.* Leicester: Troubador Publishing Ltd. Pg. 10

[53] *Auschwitz: The Nazis and the 'Final Solution'*, 2005. [DVD] Laurence Rees, UK: 2 Entertain Video.

[54] Gutman, Y (1998). *Anatomy of the Auschwitz Death Camp.* New York: Indiana University Press. Pg. 50

[55] This estimation accounts only for those killed in Nazi concentration camps.

whole or in part, a national, ethnical, racial or religious group,"[56] by this definition the Holocaust is not the largest genocide to have taken place. Professor and historian David Stannard examines the genocide of the Native Americans, estimating that close to one hundred million individuals were murdered by European colonialists.[57] In contrast to the seventeen million exterminated by the Nazis,[58] the mass killings of indigenous American Indians took the lives of many more people. As well as death toll the Holocaust is not the most rapid killing ever to occur and the concept of concentration camps existed since the 1830s, having first been most widely used by the Spanish in Cuba during the Ten Years' War in the 18th Century.[59] To debate the Holocaust on empirical claims appears to be an exercise in futility. Psychologist and historian Israel Charny recommends that readers should examine scholar's writings on the Holocaust and ask whether the author uses "black-and-white argumentation to create diametrically opposed differences between different cases of genocide to the point where deaths in the one instance are claimed to be more terrible than in the other?"[60] There appears to be a contention in writings expounding the Holocaust as unique that due to the sheer horrors that occurred within it, it is somehow more brutal and unbelievable than other acts of murder.

The conceptual grounds for the Holocaust being a unique event hold much more weight than the empirical evidence. Historian Lucy Dawidowicz says that to "make Auschwitz the paradigm for universal evil is in effect to deny the historical reality that the German dictatorship had a specific intent on murdering the Jews."[61] We must be clear that we not simply speak of the 'events' of the Holocaust as we do with naturally occurring phenomena, but of the actions of willing individuals and the reality of those actions. "Auschwitz was a social and political reality. It was neither conceived nor constructed as a theatre of atrocity to play out Everyman's capacity for evil, to satisfy a universal lust for killing."[62] Dawidowicz argues that the fate of the Jews was unique. The 'Judenfrage' or 'Jewish question' referred to a sense that the existence of Jews in Germany posed a problem for the state, this defined the Jews as the 'mortal and

---

[56] Office of the United Nations High Commissioner for Human Rights. (2011). *Convention on the Prevention and Punishment of the Crime of Genocide* . Available: http://www2.ohchr.org/english/law/genocide.htm. Last accessed 16th Nov 2011.

[57] Stannard, D (1992). *American Holocaust*. Oxford: Oxford University Press. Pg. 151

[58] Niewyk, D (2000). *The Columbia Guide to the Holocaust*. West Sussex: Columbia University Press. Pg. 45

[59] Calvert, P (2010). *Terrorism, Civil War, and Revolution*. London: Continuum. Pg. 86

[60] Rosenbaum, A (2001). *Is the Holocaust Unique?*. Oxford: Westview Press. Pg. xi - xii

[61] Dawidowicz, L (1983). *The Holocaust and the Historians*. London: Harvard University Press. Pg. 15

[62] Dawidowicz, L (1983). *The Holocaust and the Historians*. London: Harvard University Press. Pg. 15

biological archenemy' and "threatened the purity and even the very existence of the 'Aryan' race."[63] It is not the scale of the killings, nor necessarily the methods by which those killings took place that distinguish the Holocaust from other genocides for Dawidowicz, but "because of the differentiative intent of the murderers and the unique effect of the murders."[64] The Holocaust was the first time that a state had operated a campaign of systematic annihilation against the Jewish race. Acts of murder had been committed against ethnic groups by states, but not against Jews and not through a total ideology to such a high degree. At the Wansee Conference in 1942 the 'Jewish question' was debated, the evidence comes mainly from minutes documented by Lieutenant Colonel Adolf Eichmann and has many omissions, making it hard to understand what took place in its entirety. The debate spoke of 'increased emigration' of the Jews and expulsion to be made more efficient "to cleanse German living space of Jews."[65] Euphemistic language, such as describing the deaths of those forced into labour camp as being due to 'natural causes', make the document difficult to draw hard evidence from. It is never stated that the intention of Nazi Germany was to eradicate every single Jew from existence. It is this proposal which could make the Holocaust unique, however it seems asinine and arbitrary to search for such a statement considering the legacy the Nazis left behind. It appears extremely likely that given the opportunity Nazi Germany would have eradicated as many of those it deemed unworthy of life as it could have. Even if this assumption were true the Holocaust would still be contended by genocides such as Rwanada whereby massacres were committed with the intention of entirely eradicating racial groups.

Social scientist Erwin Haeberle argues that homosexuals in Nazi Germany were persecuted as severely as any other minority group. Attacks were orchestrated against institutions operated by or sympathetic to homosexuality, and legally the sexuality became punishable, Paragraph 175 forbid homosexual acts even to the point of kissing or 'inappropriate' visual contact.[66] The Romani people of Europe, Sinti population, Communists and those of Slavic descent also received extremely brutal treatment from the Nazis. To say that the Holocaust was an entirely Jewish experience is to neglect that millions of individuals from other ethnic groups suffered. Those of Jewish descent

[63] Dawidowicz, L (1983). *The Holocaust and the Historians*. London: Harvard University Press. Pg. 11
[64] Dawidowicz, L (1983). *The Holocaust and the Historians*. London: Harvard University Press. Pg. 14
[65] *The Wansee Protocol*. (1942). Available: http://writing.upenn.edu/~afilreis/Holocaust/wansee-transcript.html. Last accessed 17th Nov 2011.
[66] Duberman, M (1991). *Hidden from History: Reclaiming the Gay and Lesbian Past*. London: Penguin Books. Pg. 370

do make up the majority of the death toll for the victims of the Holocaust, but this is due to the territories into which the Germans invaded and the proportion of the population they made up those areas.

Philosopher Bob Brecher puts it that "the Holocaust marks something definitive about the twentieth century."[67] He argues that it is not unique, although we should not let that diminish its radical horror, but instead it is 'unprecedented,'[68] meaning that its scale and origins make it something that was never known or done before. The 'unprecedented' thesis allows us not to become troubled with the semantics of what the Holocaust entailed but understand it as a rupture in anthropogenic history. We can debate *how* certain acts were committed and *who* committed them, but the Holocaust really asks questions of *how could* individuals commit the acts they did? The Holocaust could be seen as unique because it is simply beyond human comprehension. A well-industrialised Western European nation with a tradition of influential philosophers allowing a vehemently destructive and subsuming ideology to organise thousands of people seems inconceivable in retrospect. Brecher argues that the Nazis acted "utterly irrationally,"[69] as they directed resources away from the war effort in order to exterminate as many people as possible in the labour and death camps across Eastern Europe in a vehement pursuit of their ideology.

To examine the Holocaust is either intended to "pay proper respect and do justice to those to whom things were done"[70] or to hope, in vain, that understanding its horrors will allow us to prevent similar events from occurring again. It is highly motivated with moral and political issues considering the formation of the state of Israel, post-war reparations and the rise of the far right following 1945. Historian Deborah Lipstadt argues that in the aftermath of the Holocaust it appeared that "as long as fascism could be linked with Nazism, and Nazism, in turn, could be linked with the horrors of the final Solution, then both would remain thoroughly discredited."[71] This understanding has been proven false, not only as individuals use the Holocaust as a tool to gain sympathy for a cause but also with the creation of Holocaust denial and its use amongst

---

[67] B. Brecher, 'Understanding the Holocaust: The Uniqueness Debate', Radical Philosophy 96, 1999 Pg. 17

[68] B. Brecher, 'Understanding the Holocaust: The Uniqueness Debate', Radical Philosophy 96, 1999 Pg. 21

[69] B. Brecher, 'Understanding the Holocaust: The Uniqueness Debate', Radical Philosophy 96, 1999 Pg. 18

[70] B. Brecher, 'Understanding the Holocaust: The Uniqueness Debate', Radical Philosophy 96, 1999 Pg. 20

[71] Lipstadt, D (1994). *Denying the Holocaust: The Growing Assault on Truth and Memory*. London: Penguin Books.

Nazi sympathisers.

In the immediate aftermath in 1945 the Holocaust may have seemed to have been a unique event. Unfortunately that genocide was not a singular occurrence, destruction of ethnic groups in Rwanda, Darfur, Namibia and Cambodia have shown the human being to be capable of incredibly inhumane acts. Israel Charny is correct in his assertion that the holocaust was not unique,[72] it is in many ways a crucial and unparalleled singular events but the atrocities that were committed and the reasons for their doing had occurred before. The Holocaust really asks questions of man's capacity to commit horrendous acts, it is a landmark in the prominence of death and destruction in human history.

---

[72] Rosenbaum, A (2001). *Is the Holocaust Unique?*. Oxford: Westview Press. Pg. xii

The concept of security has been extended to include economic, environmental, health, personal, community, food and political threats. Too it extends to include individuals. Is this extension is fruitful or the security concept loses all its meaning and coherence?

Introduction

"The mode of production of material life conditions the general process of social, political and intellectual life. It is not the consciousness of men that determines their existence, but their social existence that determines their consciousness."
- Karl Marx, 1859 (Marx, 2012: 2)

"A major source of objection to a free economy is precisely that it gives people what they want instead of what a particular group thinks they ought to want.
Underlying most arguments against the free market is a lack of belief in freedom itself."
- Milton Friedman, 1962 (Williamson, 2011: 49)

In 1994 global attention was drawn to the concept of Human Security when the United Nations Development Programme published *The Human Development Report*. This document argued that security issues were no longer simply a matter of state interest but that the referent object of security should be the individual. It argued "the world can never be at peace unless people have security in their daily lives" (Haq, 1994: 1). This new paradigm argued that security issues should be expanded beyond the archetypal national security of the Cold War to include various other forms of protection for the individual including economic, personal and political security. These new elements aimed to "reflect the basic needs of human security" (Jolly, 2006: 4) and provide a better understanding for how to reach and maintain global stability.

In 2005 Secretary-General Kofi Annan claimed the UN's three key goals were security, development and human rights. This revised structure encompassed the three pillars of the Human Security concept: "freedom from want (a shared vision of development), freedom from fear (a vision of collective security) and freedom to live in dignity (under the rule of law, human rights and democracy)" (Crowley, 2008: 19). What this has really meant for the United Nations as an international organisation is unclear. Although projects have been launched by the United Nations which could, and have been, linked with this newly adopted concept, a huge number of the issues it recognises are still prevalent in the contemporary world.

This essay sets to examine the relationship between Human Security, humanitarian intervention and development aid as solutions to fragile states. Despite being broad, the very approach of Human Security leads issues to be misdiagnosed and consequently for ineffective policy to be applied. It will argue that state intervention has been the practical application of the concept and this has proved to deepen the insecurities of fragile states.

1.1 Aid

The 'freedom from want' aspect of Human Security entails that "the state guarantees basic social justice which is… institutionalized in a welfare state model with a complex system of redistribution… [T]he state sets standards for every human's well-being" (Chenoy & Tadjbakhsh, 2007: 168). Miller argues that the pitfalls of a libertarian or anarchistic society stem from the need for public goods, which means, "we need political authority with the power to compel in order to ensure that these goods are provided" (Miller, 2003). A balance needs to be maintained between the public and private sectors to benefit all; but the market cannot *replace* political authority. What Human Security misses is that insecurity could be resolved through the kinds of political authority a society has and what their limits are.

McCormack argues that "an overview of current human security policies and projects represent little more than a jumble of charitable interventions led by current Western preoccupations and wrapped up in highly moral and grand rhetoric" (McCormack, 2011: 254). The expansive nature of Human Security, including everything from air pollution to political repression, domestic abuse to the overall availability of food, gives license for states to act when they deem a 'security' is being breeched.

"The protection role stems from both an ethical responsibility towards the well-being of individuals whose rights have been systematically violated as well as a functional responsibility, given that threats are increasingly inter-linked across borders and regions" (Chenoy & Tadjbakhsh, 2007: 146).

The Human Security concept grew out of a belief that liberal market economics as a path to universal economic growth had failed against the continuing human rights abuses following the Cold War and the majority of the global population was not seeing the benefits of globalisation (Thomas, 2001: 167-168).

"Liberal values such as open societies and open markets, although intended to lift millions out of poverty while setting them on paths towards 'freedom and liberty', are also marred by increasing gaps between the haves and the have-nots, with the silent majorities becoming more distant and marginal… The uneven pace of economic growth… has resulted in major economic disparities that have increased over time and caused economic insecurities" (Chenoy & Tadjbakhsh, 2007: 12-13).

The solution it appears, at least in practice, has been a moral bolstering of the role of the state. By necessitating the state to intervene in the affairs of other sovereign states when there are occurrences that violate the security of citizens, Human Security invariable leads to humanitarian intervention in its various forms. One such form, readily adopted by the West is the manipulation of foreign economies with development aid.

1.2 Fragile States and Aid

In *The World Development Report 2012* thirty-four states were identified by the World Bank as being 'fragile states' (World Bank, 2012), of these, nineteen of them are located in Africa, the poorest inhabited continent in the world (Smith, 2011). Since 1960 $1 trillion in development-related aid has been transferred from wealthy nations to Africa, with much of it coming from campaigns such as Make Poverty History and Live 8, the adoption of the United Nations Millennium Declaration,[73] and the creation of bodies such as the African Commission on Human and Peoples' Rights (Moyo, 2009a: xviii). Despite this incredible redistribution of wealth, "more than 50% of the population - over 350 million people - live on less than a dollar a day, a figure that has nearly doubled in two decades" (Moyo, 2009b). In 2012 the United States alone donated over $58.6 million to Angola (Foreign Assistance Office, 2012), a country that in October the same year witnessed an increase in the percentage of the population living in extreme poverty (Tran, 2012). The classic portrayal of development aid is that it targets 'underdeveloped' or 'fragile states' that desperately need financial support to protect citizens and encourage economic growth. Although this approach appears to be of necessity, and almost exhibits altruism, the harsh reality is that development aid is failing to achieve its goals of poverty reduction.

In 2000, one hundred and eighty-nine countries agreed to achieve the Millennium Development Goals (MDGs) established following the Millennium Summit in New York City. This eight-point action plan was aimed at education, gender equality, lowering child mortality rates, combating diseases including HIV/AIDS, the environment and alleviating poverty and hunger. A deadline of 2015 was set to achieve these objectives but progress has been slow and uneven. In 2005, after an assessment by the UN predicted that targets would fail to be met, donors agreed to increase their funding to developing nations from $80 billion to $130 billion by 2010 (WFUNA,

---

[73] Including the Millennium Development Goals.

2012). In 2011 researchers at *The Lancet* projected that only nine of the one hundred and thirty-seven developing countries accounted for by the initiative will achieve the goal of reducing child mortality rates by 2015, and twenty-three countries in Sub-Saharan Africa are unlikely to achieve it before 2040 (Dreaper, 2011). Since the adoption of the goals the number of women dying during childbirth is still in the hundreds of thousands, a figure substantially higher than the UN goal had hoped to prevent and world hunger rates have actually increased (Plett, 2010). It is not to say that there is no room for failure when attempting to accomplish the Millennium Development Goals but rather efforts have been wasted, for there are clearer and far more efficient ways of alleviating poverty than collecting from taxpayers to fund government-mandated programmes which yield poor results.

For example, the first target of the MDG initiative was to halve, between 1990 and 2015, the proportion of people who live on less than $1 per day (United Nations, 2012) and it looks as if this outcome largely will occur. However, this is not due to the enormous financing the initiative has taken, but is down to robust economic growth in China and India (BBC, 2010), which has come from real capital investment. China has opened its doors to private financing with minimal levels of regulation and the advantage of a labour force which can vastly undercut that of 'more developed' nations in the West. This process has "lifted some half a billion people out of poverty over the past three decades and rapidly created the world's largest middle class to provide an engine for long-term domestic consumer demand" (Karon, 2011). India too is reaping the benefits of its decision to liberalise the economy. In the first three decades after independence, when the government conducted a system of central planning, GDP per capita grew only by 1.25%. Since the 1990s it has accelerated to 7.25%, a figure that will see average income double in the next decade (OECD, 2007), a factor that will lead to poverty reduction in absolute terms. The reason for this rapid growth has come from the removal or easing of government regulation, in the last two decades, on industries such as communication, asset management and information technology. "In those infrastructure sectors which have been opened to competition… the private sector has proven to be extremely effective and growth has been phenomenal" (OECD, 2007). By rolling back government and allowing the private sector forces to take control of the economy, there has been a boom in the creation of the real material wealth Indian citizens require for a decent standard of living. India has now emerged as one of the newly coined 'BRICS', a group of five countries with rapidly expanding economies that currently attract 53% of all financial global capital (Baruah, 2012). Much of the long-term progress that has been made in Africa has come from investment in basic physical and organisational structures. Of the $72 billion invested in the infrastructure of the African continent every year, 29% (a staggering $21 billion) is accounted for solely by telecommunications (Sassoulas, 2012). To attract foreign direct investment it is critical a country has a robust, modern communications system by which people can organise. In Ethiopia aid constitutes more than 90% of the government budget yet only 2% of the country's total population has access to a mobile phone (Moyo, 2009b). The government of Ethiopia holds a monopoly on the telecommunications market, allowing only one company, Ethiopian Telecommunications Corporation[74] to operate. Foreign SIM cards pay premium rates, or are entirely unable to connect to the network and this causing hesitance in outside companies to investment. To spur economic activity would it not seem reasonable for the government to allow private citizens the license to create their own mobile telecommunications networks? What the state desperately needs to do is to allow those citizens who can, the possibility of starting businesses that will then go on to further spur economic activity and foster stability.

1.3 Aid and Conflict

Bauer argues that the term 'aid' being used to describe transfers of wealth creates an unquestioning attitude:

"It disarms criticism, obscures realities, and prejudges results. Who can be against aid to the less fortunate? The term has enabled aid supporters to claim a monopoly of compassion and to dismiss critics as lacking in understanding and compassion" (2004).

Blanchette argues that foreign aid is "a system through which political power becomes entrenched, political favors are distributed, enemies are punished. And despite its record of unmitigated failure, foreign aid… has grown both in size and scope" (2003). Although aid can often have questionable motives such as the financial support the United States provides to Israel, despite it holding the 17th highest Human Development Index rating in the world (UNDP, 2011: 127-130), it generally appears to have sincere and positive intentions. Reducing the amount of poverty in the world to

---

[74] Recently rebranded Ethio Telecom.

alleviate human suffering is a noble cause, but foreign aid is not the solution and its implementation can in fact have the reverse effect. Moyo argues in *Dead Aid* that development aid is an abettor to corruption, and props up corrupt governments by providing them with a never-ending supply of freely usable money:

"Corrupt governments interfere with the rule of law, the establishment of transparent civil institutions and the protection of civil liberties, making both domestic and foreign investment in poor countries unattractive. Greater opacity and fewer investments reduce economic growth, which leads to fewer job opportunities and increasing poverty levels. In response to growing poverty, donors give more aid, which continues the downward spiral of poverty" (2009a: 49).

For long-term sustainable development a well-functioning civil society and politically involved citizenry are crucial. In functioning, healthy economies the process of a government taxing its citizens for public services should lead to government accountability. By circumventing this process, aid causes a reduction in the dependence of government on its citizenry, in effect "it owes its people nothing" (Moyo, 2009a: 58). The evidence of this has been the sluggish lowering of poverty rates in African nations that receive high levels of aid, compounded by numerous instances of embezzlement and corruption on a vast scale. One of the most notorious perpetrators is President Mobutu Sese Seko, who stole approximately $5 billion during his rule of Zaire,[75] roughly 40% of all the foreign aid his government received in his thirty-two year reign (BBC, 2004). In 1983, directly after a meeting with President Ronald Reagan to discuss the easing of a $4.5 billion debt repayment, Mobutu leased airliner Concorde to fly his daughter to her wedding in the Ivory Coast (Brooke, 1987). The reason Zaire suffered so terribly under his reign was that:

"By nationalising foreign companies and forcing European investors out of the country, [Seko] precipitated an economic slump which was further exacerbated by unrestrained siphoning of public money to fund his extravagant Concorde and Mercedes-Benz littered lifestyle." (Cook, 2010).

Kasper argues, "huge aid flows to Africa have only rewarded incompetent despots and kleptocratic elites, whereas absolute poverty has plummeted in India and China, countries which have received comparatively little foreign aid" (2012).

In 1967 the Nigerian Civil War erupted when provinces in the south-east attempted to succeed and form their own state, the Republic of Biafra. By spring 1968 a famine had

---

[75] The Democratic Republic of Congo since 1997

broken out taking the lives of thousands of citizens. The Biafran government claimed that Nigeria was using tactics of starvation and genocide to win the war, and called upon the outside world to help them limit the effects of the humanitarian disaster occurring in the region. The year the war started the International Committee of the Red Cross had a total annual budget of just half a million dollars. Only a year later, when the humanitarian disaster was underway, the Red Cross was spending approximately a million and a half dollars a month in Biafra alone (Gourevitch, 2010). In 1970, after a final offensive operation, the war ended with Nigerian leader General Yakubu Gowon announcing his government's victory over Biafra. There was rapid reconciliation between the two sides in the aftermath and the suffering of the Biafran people quickly stopped. In retrospect it is clear that Biafra was never going to be able to successfully break away from Nigeria, a state that had overwhelming military power as well as enormous support from its former colonial power Great Britain. Aid supplies fell into the hands of those committing atrocities, and sustained groups that without support would have surrendered far earlier (Anthony, 2010). The aid had unintentionally prolonged the conflict, leading to increased levels of human suffering and loss of life. De Waal argues:

"It became quite clear when the record was assessed that the Biafran war had gone on a couple of years longer than it need have done. One of the things that sustained that war was the humanitarian effort, and that is a very, very difficult conclusion to draw ethically for those agencies that were involved in it" (*The Trouble with Aid*, 2012).

The Nigerian Civil War is by no means the only example of development aid perpetuating conflict. In the early 1980s allegations were levied against the charity super group 'Band Aid' when it was revealed that funds raised for anti-poverty efforts in Ethiopia had been subverted, either personally benefitting members of the Tigrayan rebel insurgency or been used to purchase weaponry that in turn exacerbated the conflict. A humanitarian disaster that had been presented as the consequence of drought was in fact, in large part, the result of government policies that aimed to starve the northern regions of the country where rebel forces were trying to gain independence. Aregawi Berhea, former commander of the rebel movement, estimated that only 5% of the $100 million his group received actually went to the starving (Plaut, 2010). Although some of the food did save thousands of lives in the refugee camps, much of the aid being provided was being used by the Ethiopian regime to fight its wars. Aid sustained the conflict causing further sanctioning on the northern regions, which in turn worsened the famine. De Waal argues:

"Vast amounts of aid rushed in. But a lot of food aid into that situation without adequate control and monitoring, which is what happened, you end up aiding and abetting a counter-insurgency strategy. And indeed feeding a lot of that army, and that's actually what happened" (*The Trouble with Aid*, 2012).

1.4 Economic Growth

Chenoy and Tadjbakhsh write, "human security, as well as peace and stability, require a different set of tools and policies than economic-growth only agendas. To create economic stability and ensure 'downturn with security', human security requires social safety nets" (2007: 178). If these social safety nets come in the form of development aid, with the intention of global stability, Human Security may be misunderstanding the solution. Fiona Terry, former-Director of Research at Médecins Sans Frontières spoke bluntly of aid agencies in 2012, claiming:

"The primary motivation of most aid organisations is self-preservation. They have to because there is this overweening belief that 'we have to be present to save these lives, we are doing good around the world'. And you can't question that belief even within most organisations because this is the belief you have to sell. So negative messages, messages about the complexity of aid operations, messages… that sometimes aid does more harm than good are not ones that 99.9% of aid organisations are going to ever discuss" (*The Trouble with Aid*, 2012).

If coercive wealth redistribution by the state stalls or even reverses progress in regions that desperately need solutions, then the Human Security approach regarding aid or intervention will ultimately fail in its endeavours to bring stability to fragile states.

To enact policy Human Security invariably relies upon the power of the state, which is why the concept has naturally been so readily adopted by the United Nations. "It stands to reason that where government does not own the means of production, and simply purchases the wealth it requires… it must call upon private business to provide those resources" (Molden, 2012: 15). Revenue for projects such as foreign aid and humanitarian intervention are collected by the state from the citizenry. However, if foreign aid is inherently doomed to failure, and can in fact extend and deepen the damage done by conflict, the Human Security concept is undermined in its ability rectify the situation. It will take real economic growth, like that seen in India, China,

South Africa and Brazil, to bring stability to regions that suffer so terribly due to a scarcity of the materials for a basic standard of living. Individuals cannot be politically empowered if they firstly do not have food to eat, they cannot have concern for their environment if they are trapped in perpetual conflict.

The success story of Botswana is compelling evidence that a move away from aid towards stable economic growth not only can happen but also radically improves the lives of real people. Botswana did receive foreign assistance in the 1960s, but aid was not responsible for the country having one of the highest growth rates in the world, which it sustained for thirty-three years. It was vigorous economic reform that boosted the nation so rapidly, "trade policy left the economy open to competition, monetary policy was kept stable and the country maintained fiscal discipline… Botswana succeeded by ceasing to depend of aid" (Moyo, 2009: 38). President Seretse Khama's policies turned one of Africa's poorest nations into one of the fastest-growing economies on the continent with a standard of living roughly comparable to Turkey or Mexico (Cook, 2010). Careful management of the nations natural resources coupled with attracting investment from around the world by demonstrating its benefits has lead to development. "Textiles, agriculture, tourism, and the financial services sector all offer new opportunities for growth" (Biles, 2005). Moyo describes aid dependence as a deterrent to outside investors, "the stigma associated with countries relying on aid should also not be underestimated or ignored. It is the rare investor that wants to risk money in a country that is unable to stand on its own feet and manage its own affairs in a sustainable way" (Moyo, 2009b). Governor at the Bank of Botswan, Linah Mohohlo, argues, "Botswana's exceptional record of growth derives first and foremost from the sound, growth promoting economic policies which the country pursued" (2012). The country gained monetary independence after 1976 and the central bank insured that inflation was low,[76] budget deficits were kept within reasonable limits and total public expenditure was limited. Mohohlo claims that economic development can be replicated in similar settings by following simple rules, amongst them: "adherence to democracy and good governance… disciplined and prudent macroeconomic management… [and] international goodwill" (2012).

Goldstone identifies the "two general qualities that states must possess to remain stable – *effectiveness* and *legitimacy*" (Starr, 2009: 5). It is imperative for a healthy, flourishing society that a rule of law is established in which government protects

---

[76] A process which maintained purchasing power for the citizens.

property rights and is accountable to its people. Aid circumvents this process, prolongs conflict, supports authoritarian governments and fails to address the fundamental problems a society is suffering from. Human Security attempts to enhance security for all, intervening where it believes most suitable, and even looks at the option of using state-administered force to change policy that infringes upon its core beliefs. It takes organic change, within the affected stated, to bring about economic growth and a transition to stability. If aid doesn't work then the current practical use of the Human Security, by organisations such as the UN is attenuated.

2.1 Humanitarian Intervention

Human Security understands well the "inter-dependency of nations and individuals" (Chenoy & Tadjbakhsh, 2007: 11); it is born of the very notion that security is not merely a matter of national interest. No issue can stand alone, or minimise its impacts, as the nature of global inequality is understood as an enormous interrelated set of bodies competing for a diverse range of outcomes. Its pluralist nature blends in nicely with modern democracy, identifying the need for forums to be established that allow competing groups to be diplomatic. The problem with Human Security is that in effect it is always statist, believing ultimately that government should play a decisive role in both economic and social policy. The 'freedom form fear' aspect means that not only are states bound to protect their population from external threats (Chenoy & Tadjbakhsh, 2007: 168), but too are obliged to intervene when they deem the population of another state is under threat, with particular emphasis on human rights. The structures in place at the United Nations are the ideal embodiment of this ideology, an arena in which states can subscribe to legislation that further empowers them to intervene in social policy.

2.2 Operation Iraqi Freedom

In January 2009 President George W. Bush gave the annual State of the Union address, stating, "the gravest danger facing America and the world, is outlaw regimes that seek and possess nuclear, chemical, and biological weapons" (BBC, 2003). Not only was the intervention in Iraq undertaken to defend the citizens of the United States, who were supposedly under threat, but too it was justified on humanitarian terms. President Saddam Hussein was frequently portrayed by the US government as a malevolent dictator whose regime was callously breeching human rights laws (Human Rights

Watch, 2004). The international policy formulated on the principles of the Human Security approach allows for governments to intervene in the affairs of sovereign states "for purposes which are claimed to be humanitarian or protective" (Chenoy & Tadjbakhsh, 2007: 27). In the case of Iraq, the Arab Socialist Ba'ath Party was violating human rights on a vast scale, maintaining control through methods such as a secret police network, suppression of political opposition, deportation, assassination and genocide. The issue is that there are many nations around the world under the rule of dictators or quasi-dictators where government violates international law and varying portions of the population live in fear. Pre-2003 Iraq was not the most oppressive nation in the world, nor the largest threat to global stability. Hussein and his regime were targeted under 'Operation Iraqi Freedom' for the other benefits the war would provide, "shabbier motives of imperial self-interest soon emerged" (Brazier, 2008). From the civil war that Iraq has descended into since the removal of Saddam Hussein it is clear that the intervention failed to bring freedom, democracy or stability to the region. The humanitarian element that made up the case for war was a political tactic to win favour, and goes a long way in evidencing that intervention under humanitarian pretexts can be severely abused.

2.3 Human Security and State Intervention

Under the 'freedom from fear' school of thought Human Security not only aims to protect individuals against violent conflict but also understands conflict as the result of a range of complex and interlinked inequalities. Here the paradigm breaks away from traditional understandings of security and this expansion, in theory, will find long-term solutions that get to the root of the problems they tackle. The need to address the inveterate issues of humanitarian crisis necessarily leads to the use of force by one state against another.

"By human security definition, a weak state is one that cannot implement or enforce the law, is unable to formulate and implement development policies, has ineffective institutions, cannot collect taxes and is unable to provide its citizens with the most essential public services or the means to participate in public life" (Chenoy & Tadjbakhsh, 2007: 172).

If a state is unable or unwilling to act in a way that the Human Security concept claims it must, then the possibility of intervention arises under the pretext of an international responsibility to the 'insecure' citizens of that state. "Human security is closely linked with UN institutional reform. New institutions… are more likely to take human security-related considerations into account" (Crowley & Goucha, 2008). Currently it has been departments of the United Nations adopting the ideals of the Human Security concept, ever enlarging the breadth of the state and ever narrowing the focus of the international community to the social policy level.

The difficulty with the 'freedom for fear' approach is that the ability to pick and choose which conflicts are worthy of intervention can mean the humanitarian cause becomes a reason for intervention when it suits the state best. The United Nations Responsibility to Protect (R2P) initiative is the most widely recognised use of the Human Security concept; it understands state sovereignty as a responsibility rather than a right (Iqbal, 2010). The first pillar dictates that "the State carries the primary responsibility for protecting populations from genocide, war crimes, crimes against humanity and ethnic cleansing, and their incitement" (United Nations, 2009). From this it expounds that the international community must recognise when a state does not fulfil these requirements and "has a responsibility to use appropriate diplomatic, humanitarian and other means to protect populations from these crimes" (United Nations, 2009). It is not to say that the world should simply watch as unopposed groups commit crimes against humanity, but the historical record shows that despite the principles of R2P being grounded in international law, states still choose when it is advantageous for them to laissez-faire or intervene, rather than being compelled to.

In March 2011 nationwide protests erupted in Syria with demonstrators calling for the resignation of President Bashar al-Assad and an end to the rule of the Arab Socialist Ba'ath Party. After the deployment of government troops to quell the uprising, the protests evolved into armed rebellion and the nation broke into a state of civil war. Some estimates claim that the loss of human life has surpassed 32,000 and that the ongoing conflict has already cost the country between $34 and $100 billion (News Corporation, 2012). There are fears that without action an enormous exodus of refugees from the region will place a burden on neighbouring states and potentially spark further instability (Boot & Doran, 2012). Assad's regime is explicitly contravening international law, using violent tactics that infringe on human rights and managing a campaign that endangers the lives of thousands of civilians. Radhika Coomaraswamy, UN special representative for children in armed conflict, reported, "rarely, have I seen such brutality against children as in Syria, where girls and boys are detained, tortured, executed, and used as human shields" (Al Jazeera, 2012). A human rights disaster emerges from the reports reaching the outside world, yet the international community has yet to intervene. Whether intervention is the right course of action is a different issue, but what remains is that the apprehension of UN member states to become involved and the entangled political situation delaying any possible response reflects badly on the Responsibility to Protect initiative. If states are able to ignore what should be a fundamental duty then the concept is entirely superfluous. The R2P, if it truly does what it intends to, should make it compulsory for every member state to intervene when human rights laws are violated. However, if it cannot do so, and merely acts as a guideline that is open to political manipulation, its effects become unintentional and consequently damaging.

It is not only abstinence from intervention that causes moral hazard. In 2011, following the adoption of United Nations Security Council Resolution 1973, a multi-state coalition including the United States, Canada, United Kingdom, Denmark, France, Italy and Spain, intervened in the ongoing Libyan Civil War. The resolution called for a no-fly zone and permitted "all necessary measures" (Roth, 2011) to protect civilians. The conflict lasted over seven months and no official record of casualties was kept (Dardagan, 2011). The outcome of the intervention has been controversial, with speculation as to what would of occurred had Muammar al-Gaddafi and the Libyan Arab Jamahiriya government not been removed. Criticism was also levied against the states that intervened for portraying the event as a humanitarian intervention when in fact the real impetus was the possession of Libya's vast resources such as oil and financial capital, including gold reserves worth $8.69 billion (Obel, 2011). The motives of each individual state may never be known, but what is compelling is that concurrently the Second Ivorian Civil War had initiated in Côte d'Ivoire, a nation without oil reserves and whose main resource is cocoa beans (Central Intelligence Agency, 2012). That conflict received no military intervention. Too, despite being a dictator who had come to power following a coup d'état in 1969, President Gaddafi had maintained mostly positive relations with Western nations during his forty-two year reign. In particular Gaddafi forged a strong friendship with Prime Minister Tony Blair who was paid £2 million a year as a senior adviser to US investment bank J.P. Morgan & Co. to negotiate a deal between the Libyan Investment Authority and a company called Rusal, the world's largest aluminium producer (Mendick, 2011). It appears that when it suits the British state to denounce or support authoritarian regimes is dependent on what is at stake. This behave is a microcosm for much of what occurs at the United Nations; states quick to praise the actions of other states when they are beneficial and denounce them when looking for cause to intervene.

Conclusion

The Human Development Report "shifted the focus of security from the protection of the state and its borders by military means to the protection of individuals from a wider range of threats to their well-being and security" (Jolly, p. 1, 2006). The manifestations of the Human Security concept have been seen in the adoption of policy on government level. In order for Human Security to enact, and protect individuals, it calls upon the power of the state to accelerate change. Paris argues that Human Security lacks a precise definition, existing interpretations tend to be "extraordinarily expansive and vague… which provides policymakers with little guidance in the prioritization of competing policy goals" (2001: 88). In the case of development aid to protect foreign citizens, the policy has been destructive. As a tool for maintaining political power "aid literally becomes a weapon for one faction to use against another. This usually delays the needed peace effort, by subsidizing one side over the other" (Paul, 2012: 69). In the case of humanitarian intervention, without compulsion states are still able to decide which countries to invade with the added ease of being able to justify such action on 'humanitarian' grounds.

The theoretical expansion of Human Security should render it a fruitful for framework for getting to the deep-rooted causes of global inequality. In practice, as a tool of achieving stability in fragile states, Human Security could lead away from policies that create the real economic growth required for development, towards a system that in fact rewards those very groups who cause instability.

What is the Human Security situation in Burma?

On March 30th 2011 Senior General Than Shwe signed a decree that officially dissolved the State Peace and Development Council, a military regime that had controlled Burma for the previous twenty-three years. It appeared that the struggle was over and that finally the authoritarian regime had gone. Soon after a new government was installed, one led by Thein Sein, a politician who had served as a general in the former dictatorship, validating the amounting evidence that the political change in Burma was in name only. Years of oppression had not ended; the devil just had a new face.

The difficulties Burma was experiencing are far from over. Pervasive government controls and ineffective economic policies plague a nation that due to comparative advantage should be thriving from its wealth of resources.

The nation struggles with the consequences of a colonial past. The British Empire, seeking the teak, oil and rubies of Myanmar justified the Third Anglo-Burmese War of 1885 by claiming that the ruling King, Thibaw Min, was a despot who wanted French influence in the region. After the conflict ended the country was renamed Burma and incorporated into the British Raj. Despite an end to the war, internal violent resistance persisted for a further five years until the occupying forces began a campaign of terror, including the systematic destruction of villages, to halt guerrilla activity. Not only did the colonial period see freedoms restricted for the general population, but a rapid pillaging of the nations natural resources.

Twenty-four years after independence, in 1962, the Burma Socialist Programme Party seized power. The political party, the only one allowed to exist in Burma at that time, was founded on the Burmese Way to Socialism ideology; a practice which meant the military being at the core of the decision-making process. It wished to expand itself, create a socialist economy and construct a national identity to unify its many disparate ethnic minorities. It rapidly descended into a highly totalitarian regime. The economy collapsed, standards of living plummeted and despite pleas from charities the state ruled that only government-to-government cash transfers could be made as a form of aid. The governments deliberate attempts to resist 'Western' influence caused it to turn to the Soviet Union to train and educate its up-and-coming commanders. The situation escalated, with tight state regulation causing the black market to represent 80% of the national economy. (Aung-Thwin, 1992. 13)

By 1971 the situation had become so cataclysmic that the country was forced to seek loans from the World Bank and Asian Development Bank. Structural Adjustment plans, scheduled to last twenty years, were devised but failed to relieve the nation of its debt. By 1988 foreign debt had ballooned to $4.9 billion, about 75% of the national GDP. (Steinberg, 1997. 5)

Having existed under hundreds of years of tyranny Burma is a complex and deeply divided nation. For those living under the regimes life has been arduous, traumatising and left them in an unfortunate position. The tyrannical regime that dominated Burma's contemporary history was as a result of the division the nation had experienced under external forces from occupiers. Forcing the society to be cohesive came at the cost of a police state, but this is an understandable consequence of the terror campaigns that came before, aimed at dividing and conquering. It is unfortunate, as now Burma must look to the outside for help, after a regime that so vehemently caused suffering through isolationist and failed self-sufficiency policies.

Not only does the nation need to begin reversing the effects of its fascist economics, opening its markets to build the infrastructure necessary for a decent standard of living, but too it must heal its wounds. The Burman people, the major ethnicity within the population, are seen to dominate other groups such as the Karen, Shan, Rakhine, Rohingya and Chin. This division stifles the society progressing as a single unit, creates resentment regarding a system which could see further domination under the guise of 'democracy' and breeds an environment not conducive to alleviating human suffering. Economic sanctions and exclusion by the international community have failed to bring peace to the troubled region but dissolution of the most nationalistic aspects of the regime is the first step towards a free and safe Burma.

Is Naomi Klein correct to describe Israel as the 'Standing Disaster Apartheid State'?

"War prosperity is like the prosperity that an earthquake or a plague brings."[77]

            - Ludwig von Mises, Economist

"No matter what political reasons are given for war, the underlying reason is always economic."

            - Alan John Taylor, British Historian

On December 5th 2005 at 11.30am local time Lutfi Abu Salem, a young Palestinian man, attempted to enter the HaSharon Shopping Mall located in Netanya, a city in the north of Israel. Unable to pass through the security guards he stood at the entrance and detonated the several kilograms of explosives secured to his body, killing six people including himself and injuring forty others.[78] His suicide attack came just five months after another man had detonated explosives hidden under his clothes on a busy pedestrian crossing outside the same shopping mall. In total, ten suicide attacks using explosives took place in Israel in 2005, killing twenty-two civilians and injuring hundreds more.[79] At the end of that same year the *Israeli High-Tech & Investment Report* confirmed that Israel had become the second most represented country on the NASDAQ Stock Market.[80]

Naomi Klein argues that Israel is the 'Standing Disaster Apartheid State'. "[It] has crafted an economy that expands markedly in direct response to escalating violence… The fact that Israel continues to enjoy booming prosperity, even as it wages war against its neighbours and escalates the brutality in the occupied territories, demonstrates just how perilous it is to build an economy based on the premise of continual war and deepening disasters."[81]

Is there validity to Klein's claim? What role has Israel's investment in the Homeland Security industry had on its incentive to reach peace with the Palestinians and surrounding neighbouring nations? This essay sets to examine the relationship between the Israeli economy and the failure of the Declaration of Principles[82] beginning in

---

[77] Woods, T (2009). *Meltdown*. Washington D.C.: Regnery Publishing Inc. Pg. 106
[78] BBC News. (2005). *Five Die in Israel Suicide Blast*. Available: http://news.bbc.co.uk/1/hi/4498862.stm. Last accessed 2nd March 2012.
[79] Israel Ministry of Foreign Affairs. (2012). *Suicide and Other Bombing Attacks in Israel Since the Declaration of Principles*. Available: http://www.mfa.gov.il/MFA/Terrorism-%20Obstacle%20to%20Peace/Palestinian%20terror%20since%202000/Suicide%20and%20Other%20Bombing%20Attacks%20in%20Israel%20Since. Last accessed 2nd March 2012.
[80] Israel High-Tech & Investment Report. (2005). *Israel in Second Place in Nasdaq Listings*. Available: http://www.ishitech.co.il/1105ar5.htm. Last accessed 3rd March 2012.
[81] Klein, N (2008). *The Shock Doctrine*. 2nd ed. London: Penguin Group. Pg. 428
[82] Commonly referred to as the Oslo Accords.

1991. It will argue that Klein is correct to assert that a major factor enforcing the apartheid state is Israel's investment in security technologies.

Bob Jessop describes corporatism as "a form of state in which representation and intervention are institutionally fused in the form of 'corporations'… Thus corporations both represent the interests of their members and act as a means of implementing government policies."[83] This economic policy was realised to its fullest between 1922 and 1943 under Benito Mussolini's National Fascist Party in the Kingdom of Italy. There the state directed "predominantly privately-owned business according to four principles: unity, order, nationalism and success."[84] Its results were the monopolisation of highly lucrative industries by a minor elite favourable to the ruling political party. State regulatory bodies advanced the commercial interests of those companies that dominated industry. Although business remained primarily privately owned the market was restricted to prevent competition. The merging of government and business transpired with policy being heavily influenced by a wealthy business lobby. In 1939 almost 40% of Italy's government budget went on military spending,[85] this perpetual warfare greatly benefitted a powerful elite who provided the goods and services the state procured through its tax revenue.

Although corporatism has a "fascist historical antecedent,"[86] a very similar process has been occurring in Israel since the early 1990s. Chairman of the Federation of Israeli Chambers of Commerce, Dan Gillerman, spoke in 1993 of Israel's ability to instigate peace and become prosperous: "Israel could become just another state… or, it could become the strategic, logistic and marketing center of the whole region like a Middle Eastern Singapore or Hong Kong where multinational companies base their head offices… We are talking about an utterly different economy… Israel must act and fast to adjust or this once in a lifetime economic opportunity will be missed only for us to say: 'we could have.'"[87] Later that year, Israeli Prime Minister Yitzhak Rabin and Chairman of the Palestine Liberation Organization, Mohammed Yasser Arafat, shook hands at the Declaration of Principles signing ceremony. Klein argues "the Oslo strategy… was to push ahead with the 'peace of markets'… by flinging open borders

---

[83] Cawson, A (1986). *Corporatism and Political Theory*. Oxford: Basil Blackwell Ltd. Pg. 24
[84] *Ibid*. Pg. 23
[85] Steinberg, J (2002). *All or Nothing*. 2nd ed. London: Routledge. Pg. 189
[86] Newman, O (1981). *Challenge of Corporatism*. Wiltshire: Macmillan Publishers Ltd. Pg. ix
[87] Ben-Porat, G. (2005) "A New Middle East?: Globalization, Peace and 'Double Movement,' *International Relations* 19, No. 1. Pg. 50

and joining the globalization juggernaut, both Israelis and Palestinians were supposed to experience such concrete improvements in daily life that a more hospitable context would be created for a 'peace of flags' in the negotiations to come."[88] It appeared in the early 1990s that Israel's domestic and foreign policies were unsustainable. The nation's import and export trading was suffering from a boycott instigated by the surrounding states, and continual conflict with the Palestinians was dispelling resources without results.

In the years after the Oslo Accords nearly a million Jews from the former-Soviet Union immigrated into Israel. Many of them were skilled scientists who had maintained the Soviet side of the arms race. Many of these professionals joined the Center for Computing and Information Services;[89] a computer training service established by the Israeli Defence Force that had become one of the best schools to source highly qualified software experts. To this day the IDF proclaims that graduates will play an important role in shaping the future of the private sector and academic community.[90]

In 1995 Israel's economy took a sudden change of direction as the 'Information Technology Bubble' created soaring stock prices for computing and telecommunications. Israel invested heavily in the speculative bubble, receiving 15% of its gross domestic product from the industry. According to *BusinessWeek*, at the time, this made Israel's economy "the most tech-dependent in the world."[91] When the bubble burst in 2000 and the malinvestment indebted invested companies from around the world, Israel was hit hardest. Klein argues that the Israeli technology companies desperately needed to find a new investment project and turned to the homeland security industry as a state-of-the-art niche market.

The same year the bubble burst Israeli military spending increased 10.7%, much of it made up from cuts to the social insurance program.[92]

Eighteen months after Israel had established itself as the venture capitalist in the production of goods and services for national security, four commercial airliners were deliberately crashed into key targets across the United States killing nearly three

---

[88] Klein, N (2008). *The Shock Doctrine*. 2nd ed. London: Penguin Group. Pg. 430

[89] Commonly known as Mamram.

[90] Israel Defense Forces. (2009). *The Story Behind the IDF's Secret Computer Unit.* Available: http://dover.idf.il/IDF/English/News/today/09/12/0302.htm. Last accessed 2nd March 2012.

[91] Bloomberg BusinessWeek. 2001. *Israel's Economy: As If the Intifada Weren't Enough....* [ONLINE] Available at: http://mobile.businessweek.com/magazine/content/01_25/b3737159.htm. [Accessed 03 March 12].

[92] Minns, R. (2004). *Weapons for Pensions: How Social Security Became National Security.* Available: www.spokesmanbooks.com/Spokesman/PDF/Mins102.pdf. Last accessed 3rd March 2012.

thousand civilians. The Homeland Security industry exploded. Before the end of 2001 it had become a larger than both the global music industry and the United States' film industry combined.[93] Governments now terrified of suffering a similar fate turned to the Israeli experts for anti-terror services. "When the market for these services and devices exploded in the years after September 11, the Israeli state openly embraced a new economic vision: the growth provided by the dot-com bubble would be replaced with a homeland security boom."[94]

"Israel [is] a unique case of a society that maintains democracy under conditions of protracted war,"[95] it has only ever seen growing financial prosperity following its investment in homeland security. In 2006 Israel spent 7.30% of its gross domestic product on defence programs,[96] that same year 3,500 startup companies were created in Israel, second only that year to the United States. This has resulted in an area around Tel Aviv being dubbed 'Silicon Wadi' in the image of 'Silicon Valley' in Northern California.[97] With almost one in ten Israelis work in the high-tech sector,[98] Klein claims that Israel's development into a state pioneering the homeland security industry "has made Israel a model to be emulated in the post-9/11 market."[99] By contrast the possibility of peace has only diminished, as Israel no longer depends on its neighbours to aid its economy and benefits financially from the conflict.

Fears concerning the future of Israel have only been heightened by outspoken supporters of its political policy, among them academic Alan Dershowitz, who writes that: "One of the goals of the terrorists... is to kill as many Israelis as possible and try to frighten Israel into submission."[100] He argues that the terrorist attacks did not arise as a last resort but were the continuation of illegal and immoral acts conducted from the beginning of the conflict.[101] Whether or not his assertions are correct it is the information that he, and many others like him use to pedal the justification for the apartheid state. Klein writes that "since September 11... the media participate in a

[93] *The Shock Doctrine*, 2009. [DVD] Michael Winterbottom, United Kingdom: Renegade Pictures.
[94] Klein, N (2008). *The Shock Doctrine*. 2nd ed. London: Penguin Group. Pg. 435
[95] Lomsky-Feder, E (1999). *The Military and Militarism in Israeli Society*. New York: State University of New York Press.
[96] Central Intelligence Agency. (2012). *Middle East: Israel*. Available: https://www.cia.gov/library/publications/the-world-factbook/geos/is.html. Last accessed 2nd March 2012.
[97] Sharmila Devi. (2007). *Business as Usual*. Available: http://www.ft.com/cms/s/0/090e5dd2-e88e-11db-b2c3-000b5df10621.html?nclick_check=1#axzz1oTWtsuoR. Last accessed 2nd March 2012.
[98] Sharmila Devi. (2007). *Business as Usual*. Available: http://www.ft.com/cms/s/0/090e5dd2-e88e-11db-b2c3-000b5df10621.html?nclick_check=1#axzz1oTWtsuoR. Last accessed 2nd March 2012.
[99] Klein, N (2008). *The Shock Doctrine*. 2nd ed. London: Penguin Group. Pg. 428
[100] Dershowitz, A (2003). *The Case for Israel*. New Jersey: John Wiley & Sons Inc. Pg. 179-180
[101] *Ibid*. Pg. 143

process that confirms and reconfirms the idea that death and murder are tragic, extraordinary and intolerable in some places and banal, ordinary and unavoidable, even expected in others."[102] Where many in the Arab world view "Israeli's very existence a colonialist phenomenon,"[103] the Western world is informed that the measures that are being taken are entirely necessary. Israel is presented as a lynchpin, an ally next to the largest proven oil reserves in the world.[104] With military and economic assistance pouring into the country, Israel has "turned into a proxy for US power in the Middle East."[105]

There are currently sixty Israeli companies listed on the NASDAQ Stock Market, making it the second biggest source of foreign listings behind China.[106] The investment for a lot of these companies came at the beginning of 2012 when the United States provided Israel with $3.15 billion of 'Military Aid'. "Israel, more than any Arab nation, *earns* its financial assistance by providing the United States with invaluable intelligence information, technological advice, and a democratic presence in the Middle East."[107] The nation depends on financing its military spending through the United States, the collection of tax and domestic investment. It now has a "technologically advanced market economy"[108] and has high-technology equipment as one of its major exports. Even the Israeli West Bank barrier that began construction in 2002 has yielded its makers $2.1 billion[109] and the company has plans to provide a similar 'solution' the United States-Mexico border.

Whilst "wars and terrorist attacks have been increasing... the Tel Aviv Stock Exchange has been rising to record levels right alongside this violence."[110] Despite a poll conducted in 2011 by *The Jerusalem Post* confirming that 70% of Israeli citizens want to recognise Palestine as a state,[111] there still seems to be no sign of peace on the

---

[102] Klein, N (2002). *Fences and Windows*. London: HarperCollins Publishers Inc.

[103] Stephen Howe (2002). *Empire*. New York: Oxford University Press. Pg. 2

[104] Shadid, M (1981). *The United States and the Palestinians*. London: Croom Helm Ltd. Pg. 161

[105] Finkelstein, N (2003). *The Holocaust Industry*. 2nd ed. New York: Verso. Pg. 20

[106] Tal Barak Harif. (2011). *Nasdaq Loses 'Holy Grail' Status for Offerings: Israel Overnight*. Available: http://www.businessweek.com/news/2011-11-07/nasdaq-loses-holy-grail-status-for-offerings-israel-overnight.html. Last accessed 2nd March 2012.

[107] Dershowitz, A (2003). *The Case for Israel*. New Jersey: John Wiley & Sons Inc. Pg. 228

[108] Central Intelligence Agency. (2012). *Country Comparison: Military Expenditures*. Available: https://www.cia.gov/library/publications/the-world-factbook/rankorder/2034rank.html. Last accessed 2nd March 2012.

[109] Harms, G (2008). *The Palestine-Israel Conflict*. 2nd ed. London: Pluto Press. Pg. 176

[110] Klein, N (2008). *The Shock Doctrine*. 2nd ed. London: Penguin Group. Pg. 428

[111] Stephen Webster. (2011). *Poll: Vast Majority of Israelis Would Accept U.N. Recognizing Palestine*. Available: http://www.rawstory.com/rs/2011/09/22/poll-vast-majority-of-israelis-want-u-n-to-recognize-palestine/. Last accessed 4th Mar 2012.

horizon. Klein accepts that the reasons and consequences of the conflict are not rooted in the economy of Israel, but argues that it is one of the main 'little understood' factors "that contributed to Israel's retreat into unilateralism."[112] Otto Newman describes corporatism as "unashamedly autocratic, elitist, unitary and… exercises direct state domination."[113] This is precisely what we see in Israel as the result of its economic foundations thriving on 'low-intensity grinding conflict'.[114]

---

[112] Klein, N (2008). *The Shock Doctrine*. 2nd ed. London: Penguin Group. Pg. 430
[113] Newman, O (1981). *Challenge of Corporatism*. Wiltshire: Macmillan Publishers Ltd. Pg. 46
[114] Klein, N (2008). *The Shock Doctrine*. 2nd ed. London: Penguin Group. Pg. 441

How central to Nazi 'ideology' and policy was the Holocaust?

"We were marched into another barrack and told to queue in alphabetical order. I stood at a desk behind which sat a young Jew from Austria, as he told me while writing my name, religion and place of birth on a card.
He tattooed number 98288 on my left arm. I was now a number nothing more.
My name would never be used in the camps again."[115]
- Leon Greenman, Survivor of Birkenau Concentration Camp

Between 1940 and 1945 over a million people perished at Auschwitz-Birkenau Concentration Camp, situated 35 kilometres west of the Polish city of Kraków. The camp had originally been a dilapidated army barracks surrounding a horse-breaking yard[116] taken by the Nazis during their occupation of Poland beginning in 1939. The site had grown over those six years from its earliest conversion into a prison for critics of the Nazi regime, to the largest concentration camp in the Nazi state, with forty-five surrounding industrial 'satellite camps'[117] and gas chambers executing Jewish civilians in their thousands.

Was the Holocaust the intention of the Nazi Party and Adolf Hitler from its very origins, a vision of a Germany and Europe 'free of the Jews' that was masterminded by the highest echelons of the regime? Would it produce a better understanding to see the atrocities committed as the result of smaller incremental decisions from which control was dispersed throughout the bureaucratic systems and networks in placeThis essay will examine the two main schools of thought concerning a historiographical debate of the Holocaust. First the 'intentionalist' thesis, examining Hitler's initial anti-Semitic messages as the first point on a straight line towards the mass executions, with plans for the 'Final Solution' at the very core of Nazi ideology. Secondly this essay will look at the opposing argument, the 'functionalist' perspective, which dictates that the Holocaust was the result of the systems that were in place, allowing brutality to be rewarded and a lack of top-down policy as the catalyst for the events that occurred. Finally, the work of historian Christopher Browning will be drawn upon to forge a comprehension between the two views to fully understand how central the Holocaust was to the ideology and policy of the National Socialists.

---

[115] Greenman, L (2008). *An Englishman in Auschwitz*. Middlesex: Biddles Ltd. Pg. 44
[116] *Auschwitz: The Nazis and the 'Final Solution'*, 2005. [DVD] Laurence Rees, UK: 2 Entertain Video.
[117] Gutman, Y (1998). *Anatomy of the Auschwitz Death Camp*. New York: Indiana University Press. Pg. 50

Historian Tom Lawson defines intentionalist readings of the Holocaust as having "often been contained within the essentially biographical studies, or at least have viewed the decision making process through the prism of an individual."[118] A reading of the Holocaust in this way inevitably draws upon written documentation, especially from those in command such as the Chancellor of Germany or Heinrich Himmler, who had the power to influence and authorise the genocide. Himmler for example, the Reichsführer of the Schutzstaffel, a paramilitary organisation within the regime, had directed those who had committed many of the crimes against humanity that occurred during the Second World War. His diaries allow historians to pinpoint where he travelled and to an extent what he discussed, in an apparent search to find a moment in time in which the 'Final Solution' or the Holocaust was ordered. Following the attempted deposition of the German government in 1923, Adolf Hiter was sentenced to five years imprisonment for treason due to his admission of sole responsibility for the coup d'etat. Eventually only serving eight months, it was in this time which he wrote *Mein Kampf,* a book which combined autobiographical accounts with exposition of his own political ideology. It is this work which many 'intentionalists' draw upon when evidencing Adolf Hitler as determined from the outset to lead a mass extermination of the Jewish people. Historians like Gerald Fleming argue that following the aftermath of the Second World War, there is a direct line from Hitler's anti-Semitic beliefs displayed in his book to the liquidation of Jewish civilians.[119] Adolf Hitler writes in *Mein Kampf* of the reasons for 'the Jew' attempting to "transform himself into a German,"[120] as due to the instability of the enormous financial structures they control, which they will only be able to enjoy the benefits of if they assimilate into German society. He calls for the reader to remember the crimes 'the Jew' has committed "against the masses of the people in the course of so many centuries, how repeatedly and ruthlessly he exploited them and how he sucked out even the very marrow of their substance."[121] The intense anti-Semitism that pervades through the work is never covert. It always demonstrates 'the Jew' as a danger to the welfare of the German people, a malevolent, powerful source of destruction and a group for which there can be no peace in Europe as long as they remain. Historian Jeffrey Herf argues it was on January 30th 1939 that Hitler made his first unequivocal public threat to the

---

[118] Lawson, T (2010). *Debates on the Holocaust.* Manchester: Manchester University Press. Pg. 135
[119] Fleming, G (1992). *Hitler and the Final Solution.* New York: University of California Press. Pg. 75
[120] Hitler, A (2010). *Mein Kampf.* London: Bottom of the Hill Publishing. Pg. 269
[121] Ibid.

exterminate the Jewish race in Germany, speaking of a solution to the 'Jewish problem' and quoting "the destruction of the Jewish race in Europe".[122] In 1942 Adolf Hitler gave a speech to the Nazi Party in where he again alluded to the destruction of the Jews: "If Jewry should imagine that it could bring about an international world war to exterminate the European races, the result will not be the extermination of the European races, but the extermination of Jewry in Europe... International Jewry will be recognized in its full demonic peril; we National Socialists will see to that."[123] Even with examples such as these it is almost impossible to verify precisely who ordered the executions of Jewish civilians, when the order was made or whether it occurred at all. Adolf Hitler was careful not to put his name to any documentation pertaining to the execution of Jewish civilians, most likely as an attempt to not incriminate himself in the genocide. In the minutes recorded at The Wannsee Conference, held in January 1942, the matter of genocide was discussed but in dry bureaucratic terms, and the debate centred on the logistics of the operation and not the morality. The deliberate disguising of language at the conference does go some way towards showing a great degree of central control within the Nazi framework, rather than power being exerted from multiple individuals. Lawson declares that despite the wealth of anti-Semitic propaganda littering the history of the Nazi Party, "for the most part [intentionalist] scholars accepted that there was no one single moment of decision, where the 'Final Solution' was conceptualised and then ordered."[124] He argues that intentionalist readings of the Holocaust appear teleological in nature, beginning with murderous rhetoric and ending with mass-murder in a linear understanding which fails to account for the crucial decision-making events that took place.[125] The next understanding of the Holocaust evolved in the late 1950s and early 1960s following the military tribunals that took place at The Nuremberg Trials. Where intentionalists see the 'Final Solution' as the result of conspiratorial co-operation, Yitzhak Arad argues 'functionalism' sees it as born of chaos and conflict.[126]British historian Michael Burleigh illustrates that the Holocaust has its origins in the Nazi Germany's 'Aktion T4' euthanasia program. In the mid-1930s many German psychiatric hospitals were opened up for the general

---

[122] Adolf Hitler, January 30th 1939, 'Speech to the Reichstag marking the Sixth Anniversary of the Nazi Party's Rise to Power', *Berlin*.
[123] Adolf Hitler, November 8th 1943, 'Speech to the Nationalsozialistische Deutsche Arbeiterpartei', *Munich*.
[124] Lawson, T (2010). *Debates on the Holocaust*. Manchester: Manchester University Press. Pg. 137
[125] Ibid. Pg. 138
[126] Arad, Y (1987). *Belzec, Sobibor, Treblinka*. New York: Indiana University Press. Pg. 18 - 19

public to tour. It is here, Burleigh argues, that for the first time average citizens were allowed to become acquainted with the negative eugenics methods being used at these institutions. "Each tour culminated in a lecture by the asylum authorities illustrating, with the aid of human subjects, the symptoms of the principle psychiatric illnesses, and hence the necessity for the regime's negative eugenic methods."[127] The idea of murdering those deemed impure, Burleigh contends, came about in 1938. The political climate had changed due to ideological fanaticism so much that the parents of terminally ill or severely disabled children lobbied the Nazi state, right up to Adolf Hitler himself, to be allowed to have their children put to death.[128] Hitler answered these calls by bringing in a scheme which allowed those children to be murdered, the Reich Committee introduced the "compulsory registering of all 'malformed' new born children"[129] by the end of 1939. What began as experimentation in psychiatric hospitals across the state became a cohesive euthanasia programme in April 1941. An assortment of bureaucrats, professors and businessmen gathered in villa number four on the street of Tiergartenstraße in central Berlin to orchestrate the murders of those judged incurably sick by medical examination. The United States Holocaust Memorial Museum estimates the program took the lives of over 200,000 individuals in six years[130], either through medication, starvation or execution in gas chambers. Burleigh argues that the National Socialists' initially saw sterilisation as the solution to insuring a physically and mentally strong state, discussing the 'Law for Prevention of Hereditary Diseased Progeny' at a cabinet meeting in July 1933 and enforcing it five months later. The program went on to sterilise approximately 400,000 individuals between 1934 and 1945.[131] It reached the point it did because of incremental decisions that were made along the way, forever radicalising the program from an idea of a struggle for 'race and nation', to experimentation, sterilisation and finally annihilation. In 1939 members of the 'Adult Euthanasia Program' visited Auschwitz Concentration Camp[132] and received orders from Heinrich Himmler to select prisoners who were no longer fit to work and experiment with methods of mass-execution. This initially took the form of inhalation of carbon monoxide from exhaust fumes and a brief

---

[127] Burleigh, M (1994). *Death and Deliverance*. Kent: Pan Macmillan Ltd. Pg. 45
[128] Ibid. Pg. 97
[129] Ibid. Pg. 103
[130] United States Holocaust Memorial Museum. (2011). *Euthanasia Program*. Available: http://www.ushmm.org/wlc/en/article.php?ModuleId=10005200. Last accessed 22nd Oct 2011.
[131] Burleigh, M (1994). *Death and Deliverance*. Kent: Pan Macmillan Ltd. Pg. 61
[132] *Auschwitz: The Nazis and the 'Final Solution'*, 2005. [DVD] Laurence Rees, UK: 2 Entertain Video.

experimentation with high explosives.[133] It was SS Captain Karl Fritzsch who advised the use of Zyklon B, a cyanide-based pesticide, to execute individuals more efficiently;[134] suggesting that the initiatives of those lower down the chain of command had huge influence on the form the Holocaust took. It appears the Nazi regime's path to genocide was an accumulative process, where experimentation and radicalisation occurred due to the initiatives of various individuals. American historian Christopher Browning looks for a middle way between 'intentionalist' and 'functionalist' understandings of the Holocaust with his thesis of 'moderate functionalism'. He argues that both interpretations share common themes, including regarding the Second World War as the radicalising agent in the Nazi state. Either as a racial war, with the 'Final Solution' at its core, or as an attack upon the Jews when the Nazi state was at it's most powerful to do so, under the guise of accomplishing a doctrine which spoke of a Europe 'free of the Jew'.[135] Browning conveys the Nazi state as reaching the Holocaust through a series of judgements beginning with local efforts concerning the ghettoising of Jewish populations. Where the top-tier failed to give clear instructions to those on the ground as to what to do with these individuals, Browning argues, the Nazis effectively backed themselves into a 'blind alley'[136] where mass slaughter was the only viable solution. He doesn't neglect the role of anti-Semitism as the cause for the mobilisation of individuals to commit the horrors they did. He arrives at the idea that "the [Nazi] state was polycratic, policy did develop on the periphery; but it was also a state defined by an ideological centre which sought control over key policies."[137] It would be naïve to consider the Holocaust as purely the result of bureaucratic systems, a product of modernity that somehow created mass-slaughter whilst many didn't even realise their involvement. It is key to consider the Nazi myth of 'the Jew' as composed of "archaic religious themes and so-called modern scientific theories,"[138] as a starting point for the beliefs the German people would have held against those they imprisoned and murdered. The chaotic nature of the Nazi regime allowed the initiatives of those at the camps to be rewarded for their experimentation with prisoners, certainly being motivated by a nationally recognised notion of what the state required of them. Where

---

[133] *Ibid.*
[134] *Ibid.*
[135] Browning, C (1995). *The Path to Genocide: Essays on Launching the Final Solution.* Cambridge: Cambridge University Press. Pg. 121
[136] Lawson, T (2010). *Debates on the Holocaust.* Manchester: Manchester University Press. Pg. 141
[137] Ibid. Pg. 142
[138] Bartov, O (1999). *The Holocaust: Origins, Implementation, Aftermath.* London: Routledge. Pg. 84

the 'functionalist' perspective fails to answer what drove those individuals to mercilessly killed thousands, the 'intentionalist' perspective tells an all too simplistic story of one man propagandising an entire society to kill. Browning asserts that neither reading can "fully account for the internal contradictions of the 'Final Solution',"[139] where resources were being diverted from an invasion of the Soviet Union to aid the killing of Jewish civilians in Europe. Motivations for the Holocaust may have changed as it escalated, potentially being realised as the war the Nazis could win, becoming more central to Nazi ideology. However, it's roots remain in the experimentation that occurred during the 'Aktion T4' program, initiatives from those commanding men on the ground and an ingrained history of 'the Jew' as a "dangerous… and deadly force in history… bent on world domination, and possibly world destruction."[140]

---

[139] Lawson, T (2010). *Debates on the Holocaust*. Manchester: Manchester University Press. Pg. 141
[140] Bartov, O (1999). *The Holocaust: Origins, Implementation, Aftermath*. London: Routledge. Pg. 83

How and why is the First World War remembered today?

The First World War was the first war, up until that point, to be commemorated on such sheer scale; with so many memorials, days of dedication and rituals. It is nearly ninety-seven years since Austria-Hungary declared war on Serbia in July 1914; but Remembrance Day, for that war, and now many others, is still observed in Commonwealth countries. This essay sets to examine what forms of remembrance the First World War still takes in the United Kingdom, the function and purpose of those memorialisations, and to try to examine the relationship between people and these memorialisations in terms of a wider reason for their presence.

Ian Hislop, in a history written for The Commonwealth War Graves Commission, speaks of visiting Masnieres British Cemetery in Cambrai, France, with its ordered 'dignified headstones' carved in a "design that ensured equality in death [that] reflected the comradeship of the trenches... inscriptions that distilled the outpouring of national grief".[141] With two hundred and twenty-five dead buried there, on nearly a thousand square meters, its style is not unlike hundreds of other First World War memorial sites scattered across Europe. They stand as simple physical embodiments, made from stone, with each dead soldier being no dissimilar from any other, in a vast space that no only aims to show humility in death but emphasise the incredible amount of people buried there. For example, Tyne Cot War Graves Cemetery, a burial ground for nearly twelve thousand men who died in Ypres Salient, is so large that it can deliberately not be viewed from one single angle; to an audience it envelopes the entirety of their vision.

Edwin Lutyens was appointed as one of three principal architects, towards the end of the First World War, to be involved in designing monuments to commemorate the dead.[142] Along with the Stone of Rememberer, now apparent in nearly all large war cemeteries, he also worked on the Cenotaph, which, aside from wreaths at either end, has no carvings on the sides. Lutyens said "simplicity became synonymous with good taste"[143], almost a development of a whole new way of life. An uncomfortable position had been met whereby a feeling that a war-glorifying culture, which had created the conflict, could not compassionately commemorate it was met with the problem that post-modernism too, was inappropriate.

---

141 Summers, J. (2007). *Remembered*. London: Merrell Publishers Limited. Pg. 3
142 Skeleton, T. Gliddon, G. (2008). *Lutyens and the Great War*. London: Frances Lincoln. Pg. 7
143 Ibid., Pg. 29

In 1919 Sir Percy Fitzpatrick submitted a memo calling for a 'three minute pause' to celebrate the Armistice, an idea that has roots in South African commemoration; he spoke of the inspiration that an entire city could create just through silence. A dawning catharsis could be created through such a simple act: "when we are divided, [silence] may serve to remind us of the great things we hold in common."[144] Stewart Mottram argues this approach actually failed to address, and even suppressed, traumatic memories; as for him the silence was the antithesis of his experience of the war.[145]

In 1993 and 1998 a resurgence of public interest in the war sprang up with "poppy-wearing among the young, a popular media-orchestrated campaign to restore the long-discontinued minutes silence on Armistice Day, and vast audiences both for a plethora of television documentaries, and... bestselling novels about the war and its memory."[146] This was due to the seventy-fifth and eightieth anniversaries of the Armistice signing, with undertones of a necessity for this to take place now. "As public recognition of the traumatic experiences undergone by survivors of war has increased, so the ageing of those who lived through the wars of the early and mid-twentieth century has added an urgency and poignancy to the endeavour of collecting their testimony and reflecting on its significance."[147]

In 1998, British pop girl group, the Spice Girls, backed The Royal British Legion's poppy appeal in what could be seen as a reinvigoration of the Armistice commemoration. The idea that the last survivors of the First World War would be dead and that younger generations could become alienated from the event, asks questions of what exactly Remembrance Day necessitates.

The First World War could have been the first to be memorialised with such extremes for several reasons. Potentially, with "an average of 457 British men [being] lost each day,"[148] it saw casualties affecting people in every part of the country, either as people they knew or relatives. Those men were young as well, "70 per cent of those who served in the war were under the age of thirty, while around 40 per cent were under

---

144 Koureas, G. (2007) *Memory, Masculinity and National Identity in British Visual Culture 1914-1930: A Study of 'Unconquearable Manhood'*. Aldershot: Ashgate. Pg. 46
145 Ibid., Pg. 39
146 Ashplant, T. Dawson, G. Roper, M. (2006). *Commemorating War*. 2nd ed. New Jersey: Transaction Publishers. Pg. 4
147 Ibid., Pg. 3
148 Roper, M. (2010). *The Secret Battle: Emotional Survival in the Great War*. Manchester: Lightning Source. Pg. 4

twenty-four"[149] which saw massive grievance of parents losing their sons in a perverse child-before-parent situation.

Eric Hobsbawm argues in *Invention of Tradition* that constructed version of 'the past' are used in modern societies as a socialising process which creates cohesion between individuals, legitimates authority and creates a common culture through notions of nationalism.[150] This top-down approach is particularly visible through the media portrayal of Remembrance Day in the United Kingdom and the guests that appear to the official wreath laying. In 2010, leaders of both the major political parties showed their respects at the Cenotaph; Edward Milliband for the Labour Party and Prime Minister David Cameron for the Conservative Party. Euphemisms of death crowded the commentary of the ceremony, there was no mention of the killing that many of the soldiers had been involved in nor the civilian casualties that had occurred due to the activities governments had involvement themselves in.

Benedict Anderson puts forward the idea of 'Imagined Communities', whereby a nation begins to imagine itself and ideas that fit within that; this in turn creates 'ghostly imaginings'[151] which allow the living to see the dead as part of the same continuing national community.

Jay Winters counters both the claims made by Hobsbawm and Anderson in his book *Sites of Memory, Sites of Mourning* in which he argues for the 'bottom-up' approach in which individual grief becomes public mourning for the dead through "a universal human desire for psychological reparation of loss"[152] because the scale of death in war is so traumatic.

It is not hard to see that a nation may need to mourn such a large loss to so many people but questions need to be raised concerning the perceived memory of the war that is so prevalent in all forms of memorialisation. Johnston McMaster, a reverend ordained to the Methodist Ministry, says that "with historical memory there is often a process of 'selecting in' and 'selecting out'."[153] Certain versions of history become mythologised and a narrative is built, and dissent or non-conformity is then repressed.

---

149 Ibid., 4
150 Hobsbawm, E. (1992). *The Invention of Tradition*. Cambridge: Cambridge University Press. Pg. 33
151 Anderson, B (2006). *Imagined Communities: Reflections on the Origin and Spread of Nationalism*. 2nd ed. London: Verso Books. Pg.12
152 Ashplant, T. Dawson, G. Roper, M. (2006). *Commemorating War*. 2nd ed. New Jersey: Transaction Publishers. Pg. 8
153 Lney, G. McClure, E. (1997). *Remembrance*. Belfast: Ulster Society Publications Ltd. Pg. 156

McMaster argues that this repression is unhealthy for a society as the lack of plurality takes away critical awareness.

Only certain aspects of the war seem to be chosen to be remembered on Remembrance Day, the indication being to remember all those that killed in combat, although, for the current generation that is very likely not to be anyone they have met. It does not speak of the "internal conflicts and government oppression [that have] obliterated 170 million human beings between 1900 and 1987"[154] nor the larger political or philosophical questions about the futility of war or whether it is an inevitability.

The First World War and the Second World War dominate as the events that many of the dead being remembered fought in, as well as current wars that dominate British politics such as the War in Afghanistan or the Iraq War. But lesser-known conflicts, those which do not directly affect the United Kingdom or those which are now commonly seen as taboo fail to receive such recognition on the day. McMaster calls for a new kind of remembrance, "increasingly in our global and interdependent community we need to remember – all the millions... who have been wiped out by our Twentieth Century inhumanity... We need to remember the ultimate evil of war."[155]

Hobsbawm and Anderson are correct in their assertions about how the war is remembered today. It may have begun, as Winters advocates, a ritual built from the bottom-up, an outcry by individuals to gather and grieve but today it has become a media event, "a practice bound up with rituals of national identification... symbolic repertoire available to the nation-state for binding its citizens into a collective national identity."[156] It is used as a tool, not to question the very reasons why so many have died, but to unify a nation with all the unanswered questions becoming disrespectful taboos.

Isobel McCulloch, speaking of her thoughts about Remembrance Day, says we should "hang our heads in shame as we take a long hard look at what remembrance should really mean."[157]

---

154 Liney, G. McClure, E. (1997). *Remembrance*. Belfast: Ulster Society Publications Ltd. Pg. 146
155 Ibid., Pg.147
156 Ashplant, T. Dawson, G. Roper, M. (2006). *Commemorating War*. 2nd ed. New Jersey: Transaction Publishers. Pg. 7
157 Ibid., Pg. 143

Have we been liberated from metanarratives?

Metanarratives have come to give structure to our lives, the great stories we are told of progress towards freedom have lead, throughout history, to the welcoming of such projects as George W. Bush's War on Terror. But what exactly is a metanarrative and what role do they play in our lives? This essay sets to examine definitions of the metanarrative, the postmodernist position on them and ask if man can ever really be liberated from something intrinsic to his being.

Postmodernism is often seen as an ambiguous and contradictory term, with its origins seen as starting with Jean-François Lyotard's thoughts in *The Postmodern Condition.* Hans Bertens describes post-modernism as "several things at once... a complex of anti-modernist artistic strategies."[158] The term has proven problematic, not least because it has been "used for diametrically opposed practices in different artistic disciplines."[159] To understand postmodernity in context, for what caused it to rise, we call back to modernism, which Clement Greenberg described "in terms of a wholly autonomous aesthetic, of a radically anti-representational self-reflexivity."[160] With postmodernism the idea seems to be of purging a narrative, a rejection of the the enforced structures that determine a concepts understanding; in art, this came to light with the work of artists like Duchamp where the absurd surreality of an article is used to provoke shock due to its context. Postmodern architecture, for example, "turns away from self-absorbed and technocratic purism, and turns to the vernacular and to history."[161] in this way it is "a move towards radical aesthetic autonomy, towards pure formalism."[162]

It is not with undefined borders that postmodernism begins to be undermined, but in fact purely the way it "seeks to grasp what escapes these processes of definition and celebrates what resists or disrupts them"[163] that gives it a basis away from philosophy. Essentially "the important question is less what postmodernism 'is' or 'means' in any absolute sense, than how for whom it has functioned."[164]

Lyotard speaks of metanarratives as a distinctly modern phenomenon in which a 'grand story' is created that is legitimised through universal reason. These metanarratives are

158 Bertens, H (1994). *Idea of the Postmodern: A History.* London: Routledge. Pg. 3
159 Ibid.,
160 Ibid.,
161 Ibid., Pg. 4
162 Ibid.,
163 Malpas, S (2005). *The Postmodern: The New Critical Idiom.* Oxfordshire: Routledge. Pg. 4
164 Brooker, P (1992) *Modernism/Postmodernism.* London: Longman Group UK Ltd. Pg. 3

dangerous, in Lyotard's eyes, as, much like totalising philosophical and political systems, they deny the naturally existing ambiguity, disorder and opaqueness of human experience; they stifle freedom with their control. From a postmodern perspective, there is no objective, neutral, rationality beyond narrative; as such, any narrative that does claim to expound truth is viewed with scepticism. Lyotard argues that "the criteria regulating the 'truth claims' of knowledge derive from discrete, context-dependent 'language games' not absolute rules or standards."[165]

If Reason is to be used to legitimise narratives, and if Reason is to be viewed as much as a religion than any other, then for Lyotard these narratives are built on false premises. As such, Postmodernism seeks to resist influences that threaten to bring order, continuity and explanation to bear on the particulars of our world. In this way "knowledge only counts as such within a given discursive formation."[166]

If the metanarrative to emerge of the Enlightenment was one of rationality, progress and truth then we struggle to explain horrific events of the 20th Century. The systematic extermination of six million people in an effort to eradicate an entire race does not fit neatly into a story which advocates understanding and reasoned decision-making. There is a dark side to the Enlightenment, it excludes that which does not fit with it; it is on this premise, Lyotard argues, that anamnesis is required to examine the evils which have been done. An exercise in painfully going back through the horrors man has done to come to terms with ourselves and where our rationality has led us, so that we might better for the future.

At the core of the Enlightenment was the predication that there was one language game, one truth, an idea of freedom that everyone could ascribe too. This metanarrative, in a sense, is a myth, Habermas argues that modernity 'failed' by "allowing the totality of life to splinter into independent speciality which are left to the narrow competence of experts."[167] These new language games and islands of discourse seek only to give narratives where there are none, empowering illegitimately and corrupting a path to freedom.

It's hard to see the Enlightenment could be seen as a defining moment for metanarratives, at most it could be seen as a shift in the narrative told; an epoch in which many narratives were illustrated. Even prior to the Enlightenment it could be argued the great metanarrative was subjection of the individual to a higher being, for the sake of the soul.

---

165 Brooker, P (1992) *Modernism/Postmodernism*. London: Longman Group UK Ltd. Pg. 139
166 Bertens, H (1994). *Idea of the Postmodern: A History*. London: Routledge. Pg. 5
167 Brooker, P (1992) *Modernism/Postmodernism*. London: Longman Group UK Ltd. Pg. 141

Aristotle spoke of the idea of a search for truth, concepts of "objectivity and knowledge from the divine to the human mind,"[168] as pre-Socratic thought had attributed composition and movement of particular particles to particular 'elements' or a pure Being. "Aristotle expanded the concept of objective knowledge to account for its comprehension by us; focusing on speech they introduced to Western civilization the concept of reason, intellect or mind."[169] In these terms, to ask if we have been liberated from something that is so intrinsic to our nature seems absurd.

In *The Truth about Postmodernism* Christopher Norris argues that in an idiosyncratic sense postmodernism is 'intellectual vandalism' as it engages in "the wanton destruction of intellectual property without the ultimate aim of rebuilding on the scorched earth they leave in their wake."[170] It offers no solutions, if we are to understand the human mind as one that is perpetually in search of truth then postmodernism, and its rejection of metanarratives, seems like the antipode of how we should function. As such, from this anti-representational point of view, postmodernism could be seen to "give up on this project of self-discovery and is a (cowardly) return to pictorial narrative, to representational practices."[171] To just see the appearance, under this understanding, does not appear to give Enlightenment values a new context but actually to step backwards in terms of progress.

Postmodernists attempt to "transcend what they see as the self-imposed limitations of modernism, which in its search for autonomy and purity or for timeless, representational, truth has subjected experience to unacceptable intellectualisations and reductions."[172] Lyotard speaks of the pragmatism of language games which are a 'heterogeneity of elements' which "only give rise to institution in patches – local determinism."[173] Where this leaves the possibility of being, in a world predicated on grand narratives which allow for us to understand the smaller stories can appear incomprehensible.

For postmodernism to quell metanarratives, seems paradoxical as the objective truth is prescribes is that there are no objective truths.

168 Swanson, J (2009). *Aristotle's Politics: A Reader's Guide*. London: Continuum International Publishing Group Ltd. Pg. 3
169 Swanson, J (2009). *Aristotle's Politics: A Reader's Guide*. London: Continuum International Publishing Group Ltd. Pg. 3
170 Norris, C (1994). *The Truth About Postmodernism*. 3rd ed. Oxford: Blackwell Publishers. Pg. 9
171 Bertens, H (1994). *Idea of the Postmodern: A History*. London: Routledge. Pg. 4
172 Ibid., Pg. 5
173 Lyotard, J (1994). *The Postmodern Condition: A Report on Knowledge*. 6th ed. Manchester: Manchester University Press.

Pragmatically the postmodern critique of the Enlightenment is useful, it keeps and check and balance on our understanding of what was suppose to be a break from oppression, but fails to account for the pockets of sever human degradation.

Ultimately it seems that the metanarrative of the Enlightenment is proving true, not in a linear form but with peaks and troughs on the way; yet it is hard to disagree with postmodernism concept of knowledge, that to support its possibility there is "no reality unless testified by a consensus between partners."[174] However, as much as we reject the great metanarratives of our time, seeing certain aspects of the become more free while others suffer further oppression or believing we have seen the end of class struggle without revolution; we still replace these narratives with new ones – ones as equally entrapping.

---

174 Brooker, P (1992) *Modernism/Postmodernism*. London: Longman Group UK Ltd. Pg. 145

Bibliography

Books

Anderson, B (2006). *Imagined Communities: Reflections on the Origin and Spread of Nationalism*. 2nd ed. London: Verso Books.

Arad, Y (1987). *Belzec, Sobibor, Treblinka: The Operation Reinhard Death Camps*. New York: Indiana University Press.

Ashplant, T. Dawson, G. Roper, M. (2006). *Commemorating War*. 2nd ed. New Jersey: Transaction Publishers.

Bartov, O (1999). *The Holocaust: Origins, Implementation, Aftermath*. London: Routledge.

Bell, N; Langlands, B (2004). *The House of Osama Bin Laden*. London: Thames & Hudson Ltd.

Benchouiha, L (2006). *Primo Levi: Rewriting the Holocaust*. Leicester: Troubador Publishing Ltd.

Bertens, H (1994). *Idea of the Postmodern: A History*. London: Routledge.

Bewes, T (1997). *Cynicism and Postmodernity*. London: Verso Books.

Bird, G (1995). *IMF Lending to Developing Countries: Issues and Evidence*. London: Routledge.

Brazier, C (2008). *No-Nonsense Guide to World History*. 2nd ed. Oxford: New Internationalist Publications Ltd.

Brecher, B 'Understanding the Holocaust: The Uniqueness Debate', *Radical Philosophy* 96, 1999

Briody, D (2003). *The Iron Triangle*. New Jersey: John Wiley & Sons.

Brooker, P (1992) *Modernism/Postmodernism*. London: Longman Group UK Ltd.

Browne, R (1994). *Beyond Bretton Woods: Alternatives to the Global Economic Order*. London: Pluto Press.

Browning, C (2005). *The Origins Of The Final Solution*. London: Arrow.

Browning, C (1995). *The Path to Genocide: Essays on Launching the Final Solution*. Cambridge: Cambridge University Press.

Burleigh, M (1994). *Death and Deliverance*. Kent: Pan Macmillan Ltd.

Callinicos, A (1989). *Against Postmodernism: A Marxist Critique*. Cambridge: Polity Press.

Calvert, P (2010). *Terrorism, Civil War, and Revolution: Revolution and International Politics*. London: Continuum.

Cawson, A (1986). *Corporatism and Political Theory*. Oxford: Basil Blackwell Ltd.

Chenoy, A; Tadjbakhsh, S (2009). *Human Security: Concepts and Implications*. Oxon: Routledge.

Chossudovsky, M (1999). *The Globalisation of Poverty: Impact of IMF and World Bank Reforms*. 2nd ed. New York: Zed Books Ltd.

Collier, P; ed. Berdal, M (2000). *Greed and Grievance: Economic Agendas in Civil Wars*. New York: Lynne Rienner Publishers.

Crowley, J; Goucha, M (2008). *Rethinking Human Security*. Singapore: John Wiley & Sons Ltd.

Danaher, K (2001). *10 Reasons to Abolish the IMF and World Bank*. Washington D.C.: Seven Stories Press.

Dawidowicz, L (1983). *The Holocaust and the Historians*. London: Harvard University Press.

Dershowitz, A (2003). *The Case for Israel*. New Jersey: John Wiley & Sons Inc.

Dickinson, L (2011). *Outsourcing War and Peace: How Privatizing Foreign Affairs Threatens Core Public Values and What We Can Do About It*. Yale University: Yale University Press.

Duberman, M (1991). *Hidden from History: Reclaiming the Gay and Lesbian Past*. London: Penguin Books.

Finkelstein, N (2003). *The Holocaust Industry*. 2nd ed. New York: Verso.

Friedlander, H (1997). *The Origins of Nazi Genocide*. New York: The University of North Carolina Press.

Fleming, G (1992). *Hitler and the Final Solution*. New York: University of California Press.

Fujimura, M (2004). *Post-Conflict Reconstruction: The Afghan Economy*. Tokyo: ADBi Publishing.

Fulcher, J (2004). *Capitalism: A Very Short Introduction*. New York: Oxford University Press.

Greenman, L (2008). *An Englishman in Auschwitz*. Middlesex: Biddles Ltd.

Gregory, A. (1996) *The Silence of Memory: Armistice Day 1919-1946.* Oxford: Berg Publishers.

Griffiths, J (2011). *Afghanistan: Land of Conflict and Beauty.* London: André Deutsch Ltd.

Gutman, Y (1998). *Anatomy of the Auschwitz Death Camp.* New York: Indiana University Press.

Haldane, J (2000). *Philosophy and Public Affairs.* Cambridge: Cambridge University Press.

Harms, G (2008). *The Palestine-Israel Conflict: A Basic Introduction.* 2nd ed. London: Pluto Press.

Haq, M (1994). *Human Development Report.* New York: United Nations Development Programme.

Herf, J, *The Jewish Enemy: Nazi Propaganda During World War II and the Holocaust* (Cambridge: MA, 2006)

Hitler, A (2010). *Mein Kampf.* London: Bottom of the Hill Publishing.

Hobsbawm, E. (1992). *The Invention of Tradition.* Cambridge: Cambridge University Press.

Hopper, P (2011). *Understanding Development: Issues and Debates.* Cambridge: Polity.

Howe, S (2002). *Empire: A Very Short Introduction.* New York: Oxford University Press.

Hynek, N; Marton, P (2012). *Statebuilding in Afghanistan: Multinational Contributions to Reconstruction.* Oxon: Routledge.

Johnson, C; Leslie, J (2004). *Afghanistan: The Mirage of Peace.* New York: Palgrave Macmillan.

Jolly, R (2006). *The Human Security Framework and National Human Development Reports.* New York: United Nations Development Programme.

Kaldor, M (1998). *New and Old Wars: Organized Violence in a Global Era.* 2nd ed. London: Stanford University Press.

Kaplan, E (1990). *Postmodernism and Its Discontents: Theories, Practices.* London: Verso Books.

Khan, R (2011). *Afghanistan and Pakistan: Conflict, Extremism, and Resistance to Modernity.* Maryland: The John Hopkins University Press.

King, A. (1998) *Memorials of the Great War in Britain: The Symbolism and Politics of Remembrance*. Oxford: Berg Publishers.

Klein, N (2002). *Fences and Windows: Dispatches from the Frontlines of the Globalization Debate*. London: HarperCollins Publishers Inc.

Klein, N (2008). *The Shock Doctrine: The Rise of Disaster Capitalism*. 2nd ed. London: Penguin Group.

Koureas, G. (2007) *Memory, Masculinity and National Identity in British Visual Culture 1914-1930: A Study of 'Unconquearable Manhood'*. Aldershot: Ashgate.

Landau, R (1998). *Studying the Holocaust*. London: Routledge.

Lawson, T (2010). *Debates on the Holocaust*. Manchester: Manchester University Press.

Levi , P (2006). *Auschwitz Report*. London: Verso.

Liney, G. McClure, E. (1997). *Remembrance*. Belfast: Ulster Society Publications Ltd.

Lipstadt, D (1994). *Denying the Holocaust: The Growing Assault on Truth and Memory*. London: Penguin Books.

Loewenstein, A (2013). *Profits of Doom: How Vulture Capitalism is Swallowing the World*. Victoria: Melbourne University Publishing Limited.

Lomsky-Feder, E et al. (1999). *The Military and Militarism in Israeli Society*. New York: State University of New York Press.

Longerich, P (2004). *The Unwritten Order*. London: The History Press Ltd.

MacFarlane, S; Khong, Yuen (2006). *Human Security and the UN: A Critical History*. Indiana: Indiana University Press.

McDonough, F (2008). *The Holocaust*. London: Palgrave Macmillan.

Melman, S (1985). *The Permanent War Economy: American Capitalism in Decline*. New York: Simon & Schuster Inc.

Miller, D (2003). *Political Philosophy: A Very Short Introduction*. New York: Oxford University Press.

Misdaq, N (2006). *Afghanistan: Political Frailty and External Interference*. Oxon: Routledge.

Molden, C (2012). *What Were the Consequences of the Iraq War Contracts?*. Saarbrücken: LAP Lambert Academic Publishing.

Mommsen, H, 'The Realisation of the Unthinkable,' Michael Marrus (ed.), *The Nazi Holocaust Vol. 3* (London, 1989)

Mosley, P et al. (1995). *Aid and Power: The World Bank and Policy Based Lending, Volume 1*. London: Routledge.

Moyo, D (2009a). *Dead Aid: Why Aid Is Not Working and How There Is a Better Way for Africa*. London: Penguin Books Ltd.

Møller, B (2002). *The Political Economy of War: Privatisation and Commercialisation*. Copenhagen: Copenhagen Peace Research Institute.

Møller, B (2005). *Privatisation of Conflict, Security and War*. Copenhagen: Danish Institute for International Studies.

Naudé, W et al. (2011). *Fragile States: Causes, Costs, and Responses*. Oxford: Oxford University Press.

Neumann, M (2005). *The Case Against Israel*. Scotland: AK Press.

Newman, O (1981). *Challenge of Corporatism*. Wiltshire: Macmillan Publishers Ltd.

Niewyk, D (2000). *The Columbia Guide to the Holocaust*. West Sussex: Columbia University Press.

Nordstrom, C (2004). *Shadows of War*. Berkley: University of California Press.

Paul, R (2010). *End The Fed*. Hachette Book Group: Grand Central Publishing.

Paul, R (2011). *Liberty Defined: The 50 Essential Issues That Affect Our Freedom*. New York: Grand Central Publishing.

Peet, R (2005). *Unholy Trinity: The IMF, World Bank and WTO*. 3rd ed. New York: Zed Books Ltd.

Perkins, J (2005). *Confessions of an Economic Hit Man: The Shocking Story of How America Really Took Over the World*. London: Ebury Press.

Pilger, J (2002). *The New Rulers of the World*. London: New Left Books.

Roper, M. (2010). *The Secret Battle: Emotional Survival in the Great War*. Manchester: Lightning Source.

Rosenbaum, A (2001). *Is the Holocaust Unique?*. Oxford: Westview Press.

Rosenberg, A; G, Myers (1988). *Echoes from the Holocaust*. Philadelphia: Temple University Press.

Rothbard, M (2011). *What Has Government Done to Our Money?*. New York: Terra Libertas Limited.

Schindler, C (2010). *The Triumph of Military Zionism: Nationalism and the Origins of the Israeli Right*. London: I.B.Tauris & Co Ltd.

Shadid, M (1981). *The United States and the Palestinians*. London: Croom Helm Ltd.

Skeleton, T. Gliddon, G. (2008). *Lutyens and the Great War*. London: Frances Lincoln.

Stannard, D (1992). *American Holocaust*. Oxford: Oxford University Press.

Starr, H ed. (2009). *Dealing With Failed States: Crossing Analytic Boundaries*. New York: Routledge.

Steinberg, J (2002). *All or Nothing: The Axis and the Holocaust 1941-43*. 2nd ed. London: Routledge.

Speller, I (2008). *Understanding Modern Warfare*. Cambridge: Cambridge University Press.

Steger, M (2003). *Globalization: A Very Short Introduction*. New York: Oxford University Press.

Summers, J. (2007). *Remembered*. London: Merrell Publishers Limited.

Suskind, R (2007). *The One Percent Doctrine*. 2nd ed. London: Pocket Books.

UNDP: Human Development Reports. (2013). *Afghanistan.* Available: http://hdr.undp.org/en/countries/profiles/AFG. Last accessed 6th Dec 2013.

Wallensteen, P (2007). *Understanding Conflict Resolution*. London: SAGE Publications.

Williamson, K (2011). *The Politically Incorrect Guide to Socialism*. Washington DC: Regnery Publishing Inc.

Winter, J. (1998). *Sites of Memory, Sites of Mourning: The Great War in European Cultural History.* Cambridge: Cambridge University Press.

Woods, T (2009). *Meltdown: A Free-Market Look at Why the Stock Market Collapsed, the Economy Tanked, and the Government Bailout Will Make Things Worse.* Washington D.C.: Regnery Publishing Inc.

The World Bank (2005). *Afghanistan: State Building, Sustaining Growth, and Reducing Poverty.* Washington D.C.: The World Bank.

Tandon, Y (2008). *Ending Aid Dependence*. Oxford: Fahamu Books.

Journals

Aung-Thwin, Maureen. (1992): 'The Burmese Way to Socialism'. *Third World Quarterly: Rethinking Socialism.* (Taylor & Franers Ltd.)

Call, C; Cook, S. (2003). *On Democratization and Peacebuilding*. Global Governance. 9 (2).

De Waal, A. (2004). *Rethinking Aid*. New Economy. 11 (3).

McCormack, T. (2011). *Human Security and the Separation of Security and Development*. Conflict, Security & Development. 11 (2),

Paris, R. (2001). *Human Security: Paradigm Shift or Hot Air?* International Security. 26 (2).

Steinberg, David. (1997). 'Myanmar: The Anomalies of Politics and Economics'. *The Asia Foundation Working Paper Series*.

Internet

Al Jazeera. (2012). *UN Report Accuses Syrian Troops of Torturing and Executing Children.* Available: http://blogs.aljazeera.com/topic/syria/un-report-accuses-syrian-troops-torturing-and-executing-children-and-using-children. Last accessed 13th Dec 2012.

American University Washington D.C. – www.american.edu

Amnesty International: Human Rights in the Caribbean - www.amnesty-caribbean.org

Anthony, A. (2010). *Does Humanitarian Aid Prolong Wars?*. Available: http://www.guardian.co.uk/society/2010/apr/25/humanitarian-aid-war-linda-polman. Last accessed 10th Dec 2012.

Baruah, A. (2012). *Can Brics Rival the G7?*. Available: http://www.bbc.co.uk/news/world-asia-india-17515118. Last accessed 9th Dec 2012.

Bauer, P (2004). *From Subsistence to Exchange and Other Essays*. 2nd ed. New Jersey: Princeton University Press.

BBC News. (2004). *Suharto Tops Corruption Rankings*. Available: http://news.bbc.co.uk/2/hi/3567745.stm. Last accessed 9th Dec 2012.

BBC News. (2003). *In Quotes: Reasons for the Iraq War.* Available: http://news.bbc.co.uk/2/hi/middle_east/2948068.stm. Last accessed 11th Dec 2012.

BBC News. (2002). *Central Asia pipeline deal signed.* Available: http://news.bbc.co.uk/2/hi/south_asia/2608713.stm. Last accessed 4th Dec 2013.

BBC News. (2013a). *Afghanistan Opium Harvest at Record High - UNODC.* Available: http://www.bbc.co.uk/news/world-asia-24919056. Last accessed 3rd Dec 2013.

BBC News. (2013b). *Afghan police accused of corruption and child abuse.* Available: http://www.bbc.co.uk/news/world-us-canada-21547542. Last accessed 5th Dec 2013.

Biles, P. (2005). *Botswana: Africa's Success Story?*. Available: http://news.bbc.co.uk/2/hi/africa/4318777.stm. Last accessed 13th Dec 2012.

Blanchette, J. (2003). *Foreign Aid, Foreign Disaster*. Available: http://mises.org/daily/1212. Last accessed 8th Dec 2012.

Bloomberg BusinessWeek – www.businessweek.com

Boot, M, Doran, M. (2012). *5 Reasons to Intervene in Syria Now*. Available: http://www.nytimes.com/2012/09/27/opinion/5-reasons-to-intervene-in-syria-now.html?_r=0. Last accessed 11th Dec 2012.

Brooke, J. (1987). *Zaire, a Paradigm of Mismanagement*. Available: http://www.policynetwork.net/development/media/foreign-aid-funds-corruption-new-study-reveals. Last accessed 11th Dec 2012.

Brown, V. (2012). *Afghan National Security Forces: Afghan Corruption and the Development of an Effective Fighting Force*. Available: http://www.brookings.edu/research/testimony/2012/08/02-afghanistan-security-felbabbrown. Last accessed 1st Dec 2013.

Bush, G. (2001). *Bush Announces Strikes Against Taliban*. Available: http://www.washingtonpost.com/wp-srv/nation/specials/attacked/transcripts/bushaddress_100801.htm. Last accessed 4th Dec 2013.

Center for Strategic and International Studies. (2013). *The US Cost of the Afghan War: FY2002-FY2013*. Available: http://csis.org/files/publication/120515_US_Spending_Afghan_War_SIGAR.pdf. Last accessed 5th Dec 2013.

Central Intelligence Agency – www.cia.gov

Central Intelligence Agency. (2013). *Afghanistan*. Available: https://www.cia.gov/library/publications/the-world-factbook/geos/af.html. Last accessed 3rd Dec 2013.

Central Intelligence Agency. (2012). *Côte d'Ivoire*. Available: https://www.cia.gov/library/publications/the-world-factbook/geos/iv.html. Last accessed 13th Dec 2012.

Cohen, T. (2011). *Obama tells families of 9/11 victims that 'justice has been done'*. Available: http://edition.cnn.com/2011/POLITICS/05/02/bin.laden.white.house/. Last accessed 2nd Dec 2013.

Compton, M. (2012). *President Obama on Ending the War in Afghanistan*. Available: http://www.whitehouse.gov/blog/2012/05/01/president-obama-ending-war-afghanistan. Last accessed 3rd Dec 2013.

Congressional Research Service. (2011). *Department of Defense Contractors in Afghanistan and Iraq: Background and Analysis*. Available: www.fas.org/sgp/crs/natsec/R40764.pdf. Last accessed 11th Dec 2013.

Cook, S. (2010). *Botswana - Africa's Diamond.* Available:
http://www.guardian.co.uk/journalismcompetition/botswana-africas-diamond. Last
accessed 13th Dec 2012.

The Costs of War Project. (2014). *Afghanistan: Civilians.* Available:
http://costsofwar.org/article/afghan-civilians. Last accessed 2nd Dec 2013.

The Costs of War Project. (2013). *Growth of Corporate Power and Profiteering.*
Available: http://costsofwar.org/article/growth-corporate-power-and-profiteering. Last
accessed 2nd Dec 2013.

Dardagan, H. (2011). *Libya: The Toll Nato Didn't Count.* Available:
http://www.guardian.co.uk/commentisfree/2011/aug/29/libya-toll-nato-does-not-count.
Last accessed 14th Dec 2012.

Dreaper, J. (2011). *Millennium Development Goals on Health 'Will Not Be Met'.*
Available: http://www.bbc.co.uk/news/health-14974145. Last accessed 16th Nov 2012.

The Economist. (2003). *The Carlyle Group: C for capitalism.* Available:
http://www.economist.com/node/1875084. Last accessed 1st Dec 2013.

Eichenwald, K. (2001). *Bin Laden Family Liquidates Holdings With Carlyle Group.*
Available: http://www.nytimes.com/2001/10/26/business/bin-laden-family-liquidates-
holdings-with-carlyle-group.html. Last accessed 3rd Dec 2013.

Eloise, L. (2012). *The 25 Biggest Defense Companies In America.* Available:
http://www.businessinsider.com/top-25-us-defense-companies-2012-2?op=1. Last
accessed 6th Dec 2013.

Financial Times – www.ft.com

Foreign Assistance Office. (2012). *Foreign Assistance By Country Office.* Available:
http://foreignassistance.gov/CountryIntro.aspx. Last accessed 11th Dec 2012.

Gourevitch, P. (2010). *Can You Provide Humanitarian Aid Without Facilitating
Conflicts?.* Available:
http://www.newyorker.com/arts/critics/atlarge/2010/10/11/101011crat_atlarge_gourevi
tch. Last accessed 11th Dec 2012.

Human Rights Watch. (2004). *War in Iraq: Not a Humanitarian Intervention.*
Available: http://www.hrw.org/news/2004/01/25/war-iraq-not-humanitarian-
intervention. Last accessed 10th Dec 2012.

iCasualties. (2013). *Coalition Deaths by Nationality.* Available:
http://icasualties.org/OEF/Nationality.aspx?hndQry=US. Last accessed 5th Dec 2013.

Iqbal, Z. (2010). *Democratic Republic of Congo (DRC): MONUC's Impending
Withdrawal.* Available: http://iijd.org/index.php/news/entry/drc-monucs-impending-
withdrawal/. Last accessed 11th Dec 2012.

Isenberg, D. (2010). *Private Military Contractors as Buzz Lightyear: To Afghanistan and Beyond.* Available: http://www.huffingtonpost.com/david-isenberg/private-military-contract_b_494834.html. Last accessed 6th Dec 2013.

Israeli Defense Forces – www.idf.il

Jeffery, S. (2004). *Rumsfeld: Iraq/al-Qaida remarks 'misunderstood'.* Available: http://www.theguardian.com/world/2004/oct/05/usa.iraq. Last accessed 10th Dec 2013.

Kaldor, M. (2010). *The Wrong Kind of War.* Available: http://www.theguardian.com/commentisfree/2010/may/26/afghanistan-human-security-withdrawal. Last accessed 3rd Dec 2013.

Karon, T. (2011). *Why China Does Capitalism Better than the U.S.* Available: http://www.time.com/time/world/article/0,8599,2043235,00.html. Last accessed 10th Dec 2012.

Kasper, W. (2012). *Foreign Aid Funds Corruption New Study Reveals.* Available: http://www.policynetwork.net/development/media/foreign-aid-funds-corruption-new-study-reveals. Last accessed 10th Dec 2012.

Life and Debt - www.lifeanddebt.org

Mendick, R. (2011). *Tony Blair's Six Secret Visits to Col Gaddafi.* Available: http://www.telegraph.co.uk/news/politics/tony-blair/8787074/Tony-Blairs-six-secret-visits-to-Col-Gaddafi.html. Last accessed 12th Dec 2012.

Mallet, V. (2013). *Afghanistan's forgotten crisis: its economy.* Available: http://www.ft.com/cms/s/0/59d9a5ae-b21e-11e2-a388-00144feabdc0.html. Last accessed 6th Dec 2013.

Mohohlo, L. (2012). *Botswana's Economic Policy and Development.* Available: http://www.regjeringen.no/nb/dep/ud/kampanjer/refleks/innspill/afrika/mohohlo.html?id=533479. Last accessed 13th Dec 2012.

Moyo, D. (2009b). *Why Foreign Aid Is Hurting Africa.* Available: http://online.wsj.com/article/SB123758895999200083.html. Last accessed 11th Dec 2012.

National Priorities Project (NPP). (2014). *Cost of National Security.* Available: https://www.nationalpriorities.org/cost-of/. Last accessed 9th June 2014.

News Corporation. (2012). *Syria's Civil War Leaves its Cities, Economy and Cultural Heritage in Shambles.* Available: http://www.foxnews.com/world/2012/10/09/syria-civil-war-leaves-its-cities-economy-and-cultural-heritage-in-shambles/. Last accessed 13th Dec 2012.

Nichols, M. (2012). *Taliban raked in $400 million from diverse sources: U.N.* Available: http://www.reuters.com/article/2012/09/11/us-afghanistan-un-taliban-idUSBRE88A13Y20120911. Last accessed 4th Dec 2013.

Obel, M. (2011). *How Much Gold Does Libya Have?*. Available: http://www.ibtimes.com/how-much-gold-does-libya-have-302983. Last accessed 12th Dec 2012.

OECD: Organisation for Economic Co-operation and Development. (2007). *Economic Survey of India, 2007*. Available: www.oecd.org/india/39452196.pdf. Last accessed 10th Dec 2012.

Office of the United Nations High Commissioner for Human Rights. (2011). *Convention on the Prevention and Punishment of the Crime of Genocide*. Available: http://www2.ohchr.org/english/law/genocide.htm.

Otten, C. (2013). *Exploding Violence Threatens to Renew Civil War in Iraq*. Available: http://www.usatoday.com/story/news/world/2013/09/17/iraq-violence/2789107/. Last accessed 3rd Dec 2013.

Plaut, M. (2010). *On the Trail of Ethiopia Aid and Guns*. Available: http://news.bbc.co.uk/2/hi/programmes/from_our_own_correspondent/8548412.stm. Last accessed 16th Nov 2012.

Plett, B. (2010). *Uneven Progress of UN Millennium Development Goals*. Available: http://www.bbc.co.uk/news/world-11364717. Last accessed 10th Dec 2012.

Prado, J. (2013). *The Privatisation of War*. Available: http://www.globalresearch.ca/the-privatisation-of-war-private-security-companies-on-contract-with-un-humanitarian-and-peace-keeping-operations/5342155. Last accessed 6th Dec 2013.

Roberts, D. (2013). *Taliban peace talks: 'Peace and reconciliation' negotiations to take place in Qatar*. Available: http://www.theguardian.com/world/2013/jun/18/us-peace-talks-taliban-afghanistan. Last accessed 3rd Dec 2013.

Roston, A. (2009). *How the US Funds the Taliban*. Available: http://www.thenation.com/article/how-us-funds-taliban. Last accessed 13th Dec 2013.

Roth, R. (2011). *U.N. Security Council Approves No-Fly Zone in Libya*. Available: http://edition.cnn.com/2011/WORLD/africa/03/17/libya.civil.war/index.html?hpt=T2. Last accessed 13th Dec 2012.

Sarwary, B. (2012). *Why Taliban are so strong in Afghanistan*. Available: http://www.bbc.co.uk/news/world-asia-16851949. Last accessed 5th Dec 2013.

Sassoulas, C. (2012). *Africa: The Infrastructure that Actually Drives Growth*. Available: http://www.bbc.co.uk/news/business-18699197. Last accessed 10th Dec 2012.

Shroder, J. (2012). *Afghanistan*. Available: http://www.webcitation.org/5kwDUj6WJ. Last accessed 5th Dec 2013.

Smith, D. (2011). *Africa's Burgeoning Middle Class Brings Hope to a Continent.* Available: http://www.guardian.co.uk/world/2011/dec/25/africas-middle-class-hope-continent. Last accessed 10th Dec 2012.

SourceWatch. (2013). *Bin Laden Group.* Available: http://www.sourcewatch.org/index.php/Bin_Laden_Group. Last accessed 6th Dec 2013.

Spokesman Books - www.spokesmanbooks.com

Stanger, A. (2011). *Contractors' War.* Available: http://www.berfrois.com/2011/05/contractors-war/. Last accessed 2nd Dec 2013.

Tran, M. (2012). *Africa's Mineral Wealth Hardly Denting Poverty Levels, says World Bank.* Available: http://www.guardian.co.uk/global-development/2012/oct/05/africa-mineral-wealth-poverty-world-bank. Last accessed 11th Dec 2012.

The United Nations - www.un.org

United Nations. (2012). *Goal 1: Eradicate Extreme Poverty & Hunger.* Available: http://www.un.org/millenniumgoals/poverty.shtml. Last accessed 11th Dec 2012.

United Nations. (2009). *The Responsibility to Protect.* Available: http://www.un.org/en/preventgenocide/adviser/responsibility.shtml. Last accessed 10th Dec 2012.

United Nations Development Programme. (2011). *Human Development Report 2011.* Available: http://hdr.undp.org/en/media/HDR_2011_EN_Tables.pdf. Last accessed 9th Dec 2012.

United States Holocaust Memorial Museum. (2011). *Euthanasia Program.* http://www.ushmm.org

WFUNA: World Federation of United Nations Associations. (2012). *Millennium Development Goal #8.* Available: http://www.wfuna.org/mdg-global-partnership. Last accessed 11th Dec 2012.

World Bank Group – www.worldbank.org

The World Bank. (2013). *Military Expenditure.* Available: http://data.worldbank.org/indicator/MS.MIL.XPND.GD.ZS. Last accessed 1st Dec 2013.

World Bank. (2012). *Harmonized List of Fragile Situations Financial Year 2013.* Available: http://siteresources.worldbank.org/EXTLICUS/Resources/511777-1269623894864/FCSHarmonizedListFY13.pdf. Last accessed 11th Dec 2012.

Public Speeches

Adolf Hitler, January 30th 1939, 'Speech to the Reichstag marking the Sixth Anniversary of the Nazi Party's Rise to Power', *Berlin*.

Adolf Hitler, November 8th 1943, 'Speech to the Nationalsozialistische Deutsche Arbeiterpartei', *Munich*.

Film

Curtis, A. *All Watched Over by Machines of Loving Grace, Episode 1: Love and Power*, 2011. [DVD] UK: BBC Productions.

Rees, L. *Auschwitz: The Nazis and the 'Final Solution'*. 2005. [DVD] UK: 2 Entertain Video.

Anderson, B. *This Is What Winning Looks Like*. 2013. [Video] VICE Media.

Anderson, B. *Inside Afghanistan*. 2008. [Video] VICE Media.

Blair, F. *Afghanistan: War Without End*. 2004 [Film] BBC Films.

Earp, J. *War Made Easy*. 2008. [DVD] Media Education Foundation.

Black, S. *Life and Debt*, 2001. [DVD] USA: Tuff Gong Pictures.

Pilger, J. *The New Rulers of the World*, 2001. [DVD] UK: Carlton Television.

Rowley, R. *Dirty Wars*. 2013. [Film] Big Noise Films.

Smith, S. *The Business of War: SOFEX*. 2013. [Film] VICE Media.

Winterbottom, M *The Shock Doctrine*, 2009. [DVD] UK: Renegade Pictures.

Pollack, R. *The Trouble with Aid*, 2012. [DVD] UK: BBC Four.

Munro, D. *War By Other Means*, 1992. [DVD] UK: Central Independent Television plc.

Newspapers and Magazines

The Economist, 8th February 2003